This book is made possible through the generous support of our sponsors:

Bank of America

Chuck and Linda Barbo

Neal and Jan Dempsey

Herb and Sharon Mead

Tom and Dixie Porter

Great Games and Golden Moments

HUSKY
STADIUM

Text by W. Thomas Porter and Jim Daves
Photography by Robin Hood with Introduction by Bob Rondeau

PARKER HOOD
PRESS

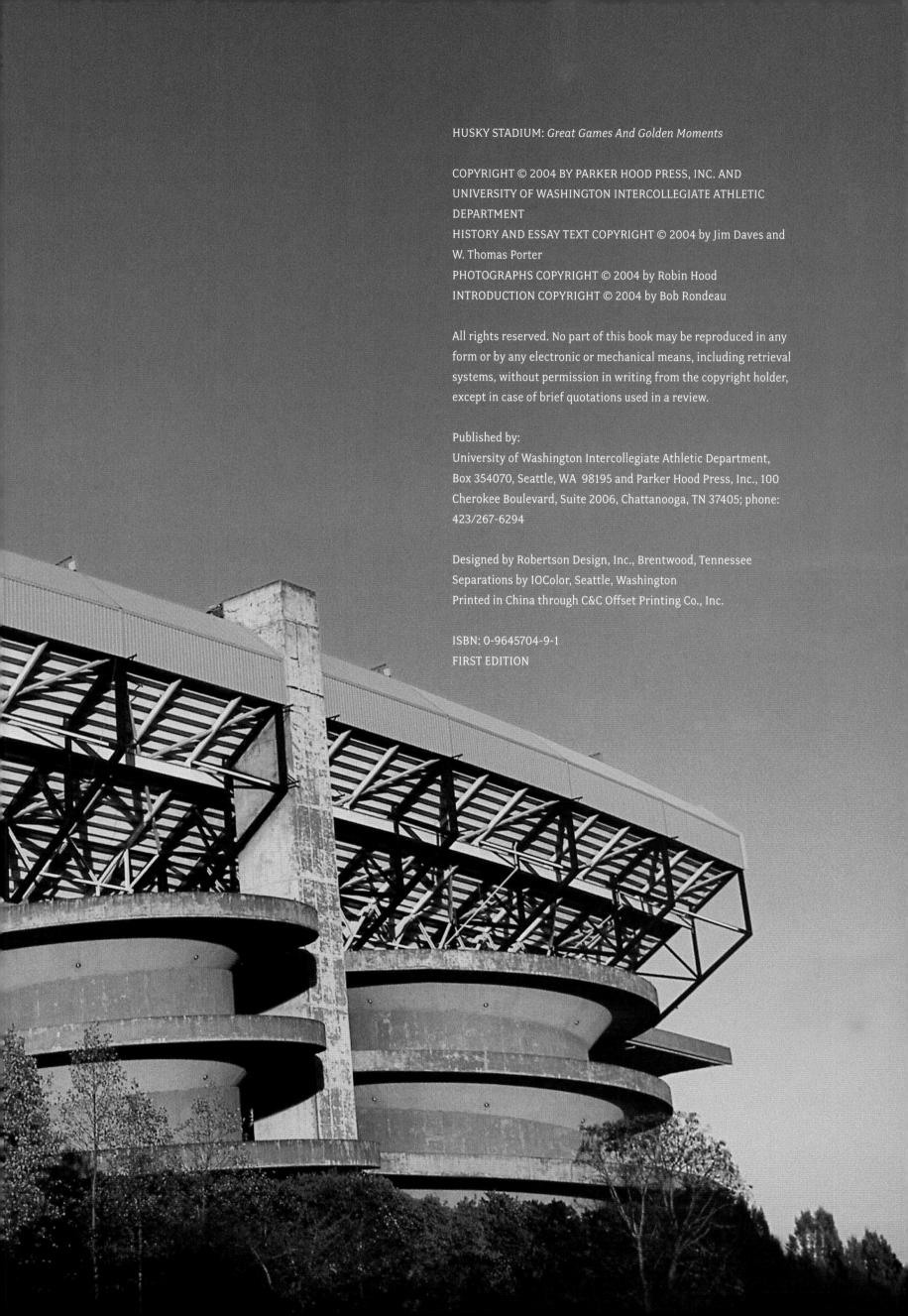

Published by:
University of Washington Intercollegiate Athletic Department,
Box 354070, Seattle, WA 98195 and Parker Hood Press, Inc., 100
Cherokee Boulevard, Suite 2006, Chattanooga, TN 37405; phone:
423/267-6294

Designed by Robertson Design, Inc., Brentwood, Tennessee
Separations by IOColor, Seattle, Washington
Printed in China through C&C Offset Printing Co., Inc.

ISBN: 0-9645704-9-1
FIRST EDITION

Great Games and Golden Moments

HUSKY STADIUM

Acknowledgments

We want to acknowledge the thousands of former and current athletes, coaches, students, faculty members and Husky fans who have given their time, resources, passion and loyalty to the Husky football program. They inspired us to write this book chronicling the people and events that have shaped the history of Husky Stadium.

Many helped us in the book's research and development. The University of Washington Athletic Department has championed this project from the start. We thank former Athletic Director Barbara Hedges, former Senior Associate Athletic Director Gary Barta, Assistant Director Chip Lydum, Marketing and Promotions Director Leslie Wurzberger, and Chris Miller, administrative assistant for external relations. The Media Relations Department has provided extraordinary support, and we thank the staff, former employees and student assistants who helped document the history of Husky football.

This project would not have been possible without the efforts of the photographers who captured historic moments in Husky Stadium through the decades. Many of their names have been lost to time, but we are indebted to the outstanding services provided by such talented individuals as Bob Peterson, Bruce Terami, Joanie Komura, Ethan Jansen, Corky Trewin, and Betty Kumpf.

We also thank the staff of the Manuscript, Special Collections and University Archives Division of the University of Washington Libraries, particularly Nicolette Bromberg and Kris Kinsey. They provided significant help in finding the appropriate archival material to support the history text in this book. Carolyn Marr of the Museum of History and Industry and Susan Pelton of the *Seattle Times* provided assistance in obtaining several archival photographs.

We are grateful to former athletes, coaches, administrators and fans who provided special input and reviewed sections of the book. They are George Briggs, Herman Brix, Chuck Carroll, Barry Erickson, Lou Gellerman, Don James, Jim Lambright, Jim McCurdy, Brad McDavid, Don McKeta, Jim Owens, Tony Piro, Rick Redman, Dick Rockne, Steve Rudman, Dick Sprague, Dean Suddath, Dave Torrell, Larry White and Ken Winstead. Special thanks go to Dr. Ray Cardwell and Dave Eskenazi, who enabled us to photograph memorabilia they collected over many years.

We thank editor Barry Parker, photographer Robin Hood and designers John Robertson and Jeff Carroll for their enormously helpful advice and professional expertise in every phase of producing this book. Tom Porter wants to extend special thanks for being able to tell his grandchildren that he just got off the phone with Robin Hood. They were very impressed.

Finally, thanks to our wives, Patti Daves and Dixie Jo Porter, who read drafts, provided wise counsel and helped in a number of important ways.

Research for this book has been done through January 2004 from information available up until that time.

—Jim Daves and Tom Porter

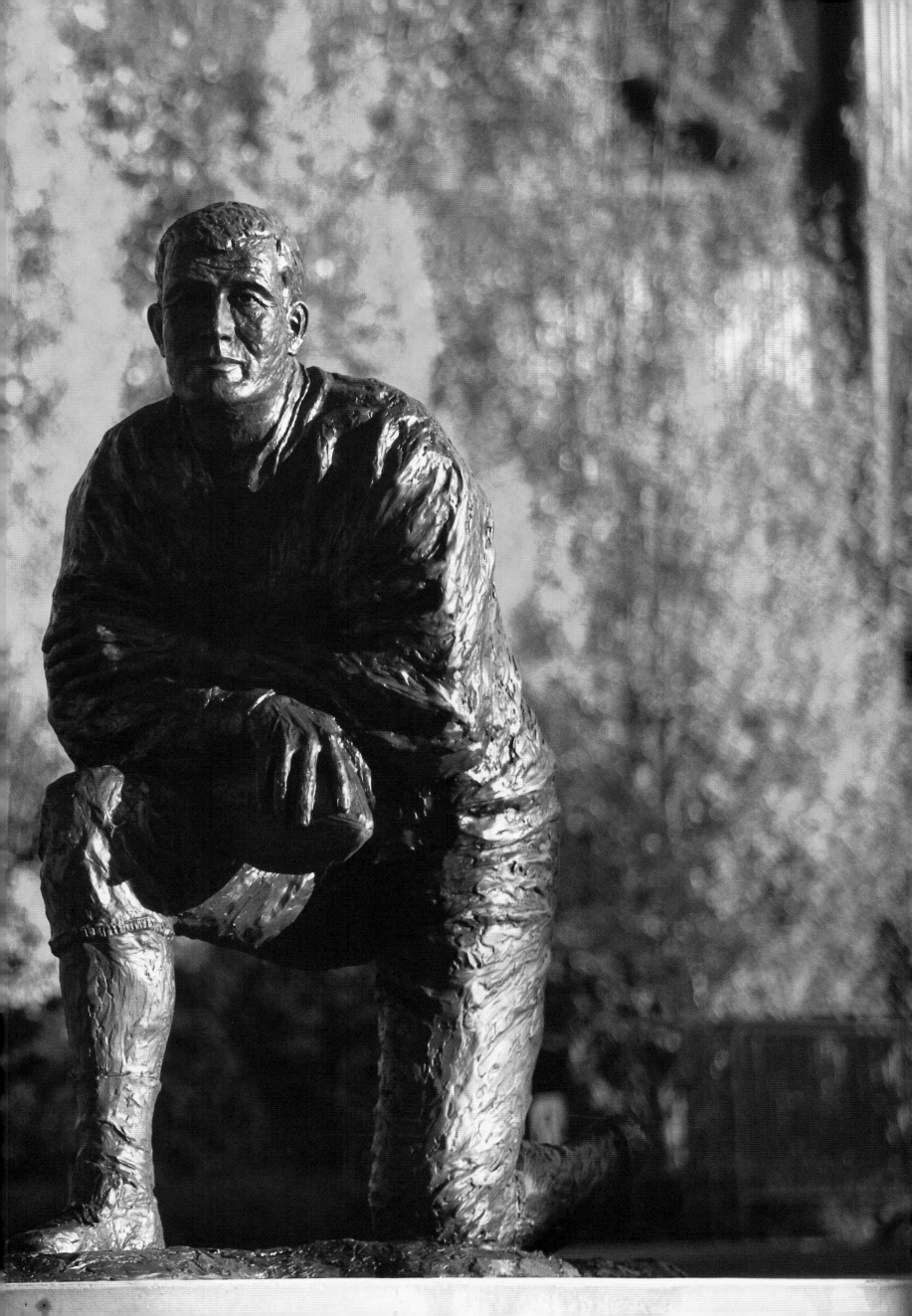

By Don James

There are numerous things that make Washington football special, and I can think of none greater than Husky Stadium. Every morning, as I drove to work from my home in Bellevue, it rose magnificently on the horizon as a monument to the Husky program.

While players and coaches and fans have come and gone, it is the one constant in our heritage.

I think Husky Stadium has a different meaning to different people. It means something different to each of the fans, the players and the coaches. For me for 18 years, it was my classroom. It was where I went to work. It was the world's best office.

During my tenure at the University of Washington, I was associated with some of the greatest teams and players in college football history. Washington is truly one of the finest academic institutions in the world and provides an outstanding environment to learn, grow and mature as an individual.

Husky Stadium is an incredible place to play a football game. Its orientation to the water and the mountains, its upper decks rising to the sky, the walk down the tunnel onto the field, and the passion of Husky fans make it one of the greatest venues for college football in all of the country.

Husky football excites, inspires and rallies students, faculty, alumni and the community around the program. They are proud of the Husky tradition. HUSKY STADIUM: *Great Games and Golden Moments* chronicles the history of this magnificent place. In text and archival pictures and memorabilia, the book captures both Husky tradition and game-day pageantry.

It helps all of us to relive the big games and big seasons and to rekindle our memories of Husky legends.

Foreword

By Jim Owens

I arrived at Washington in 1957 at age 29 to take my first head coaching job and resurrect a program that had been put on probation a year earlier. Washington had not won a Pacific Coast Conference title since 1936. The conference champion had won only one Rose Bowl game in the PCC's pact with the Big Ten winner that started in 1947. We had a lot of rebuilding to do.

The program produced some pretty remarkable teams in the late fifties and early sixties. Seattle and the Northwest embraced our back-to-back Rose Bowl champions in a very unique way. It was a wonderful experience for the players, coaches and fans.

I have played on and coached many great college football teams. But none of those teams played in a more scenic place than Husky Stadium nor in front of more passionate fans. In 18 years of coaching, I was always impressed with the attitude, determination and pride of the men who wore the purple and gold. They were fierce competitors. Sometimes the weather was not so good, the field was muddy, and the opponent was tough. But the Huskies battled every minute of every game.

There is very little in sport that compares with a classic match-up with a big collegiate opponent on a Saturday afternoon. There were many of those games during my coaching tenure. This book contains a review of those years and the other seasons that make up the rich Husky football history. In exciting text and magnificent photography, it describes not only the history of Husky Stadium but the splendor and color of game day in one of college football's most spectacular settings.

Introduction

by Bob Rondeau

Character.

It's something we talk about all the time in athletics, usually as it relates to players or to coaches. Every so often, however, we extend the discussion of character to *places*. And there is no better example than Husky Stadium.

I might get a pretty fair argument from some of the folks who sit in the upper deck across the way, but I think I have the best seat in the house when it comes to watching the spectacle of Washington football at Husky Stadium.

The radio broadcast booth where we call the action is located on the main press deck. Having spent home-game Saturdays there for more than half my lifetime, I consider myself an authority on the character of our perch. Describing it as Spartan might convey too glorious an image. There is just enough room for me, broadcast analyst Chuck Nelson, an engineer, spotters and a statistician. It's cozy, but that's fine by me.

Sitting high above the field gives us an incomparable perspective for calling the games. You have a great vantage point for following the action below. It's almost like watching an animated coaches' chalkboard.

Thanks to the way the press box is constructed, you can actually feel the energy of the crowd below. Sometimes after a big play, you get the sensation of a small earthquake rumbling upward. It's very noticeable and something I've encountered in only one other place. That was Memorial Stadium in Berkeley, California, when there really *was* an earthquake during a game. Suffice it to say, I'll take the "vibration" of Husky Stadium any day. It means something good is happening for Washington.

Like that time in 1981 when Washington was hosting third-ranked USC in a howling wind- and rainstorm. The press box was already rattling with the weather and shook even more so when the Dawgs upset the Trojans 13-3 on the way to the Rose Bowl. I can only imagine how this rock and roll must have felt to a first-time press-box visitor. It was amazing!

Indeed there have been other games where the electricity in Husky Stadium lit up a fall Saturday afternoon: Nebraska in 1992, Miami in 2000 or any Apple Cup day. But perhaps the most exciting moment in Husky Stadium history, for me at least, came in September of 1990 on a weekend celebrating the 100th year of Husky football. Again, it was a top-five-ranked USC team in town. The night before the game, I attended a function honoring members of the Husky Centennial team. Talk about character! It was tremendously exciting to see and talk with a lot of those players who shaped Washington's football history. They left some big footprints on Husky turf.

The next day, the Huskies left more than a few footprints on SC, blanking the Trojans 31-0 and serving notice of so many wins to come. This was the day Trojan quarterback Todd Marinovich would say, "All I saw was purple." Saw it and heard it, too. Husky stadium was absolutely on fire that day. When they get around to celebrating the 200th year of Husky football,

"Sometimes after a big play,

you can bet they'll still be talking about that game. What a remarkable experience.

And in the end, it is experience that shapes character. In people or in places.

That experience, for me, dates back to 1977 when I first set foot in Husky Stadium. Having grown up and gone to college in Colorado, I had come to Seattle as sports director for KOMO Radio. I was awfully impressed with the stadium from day one, although the Huskies opened that season by losing at home to Mississippi State. Not a great start but they wound up with a big finish, going to the Rose Bowl and beating Michigan.

The next year, KOMO obtained broadcast rights to Husky sports. In 1978 and 1979, I served as football analyst, with KOMO-TV's Bruce King contributing the play-by-play. When Bruce took a job in New York, I moved to play-by-play. Except for a three-year period when the Husky rights went to another station ("the dark years" as we refer to them), I've called every football game the Huskies have played since 1979 (save for the Orange Bowl after the 1984 season when a network contract prevented us from broadcasting the win over Oklahoma back to the Northwest).

Those games have produced countless memories of players and plays, of sights and sounds and emotions. And no, they're not "frozen in time." They are very much alive. And I become that much more alive in recounting them, not to mention anticipating what the next game will bring. I'm sure all Husky fans have such memory banks, some more extensive than others depending on one's longevity and history at Husky Stadium.

Mention "the leap by the lake," and Husky followers will leap to attention recalling an incredible play by Arizona quarterback Ortege Jenkins in a last-minute Wildcat win in Seattle in 1998 that left 70,000-plus gasping in unison. Or how about the two-point conversion pass from Steve Pelluer to a relatively unknown tight end named Larry Michael for a one-point win over Michigan in the 1983 home opener? I remember shaking like a leaf before that play and saying on the air: "It's way too early in the season to be feeling like this!"

As for the players making the plays, again I'm sure we all have our favorites. Mine would include Steve Emtman, the finest football player I've ever seen. Jacque Robinson might have been a problem child in practice every so often, but when game day came, you knew the shifty running back would be at his best. Chuck Nelson is one of the greatest kickers in college football

you get the sensation *of a small* earthquake *rumbling upward."*

history and a valued colleague and friend today. And Marques Tuiasosopo will always have a place in our hearts for his unwavering leadership. It's ironic that our very first Husky broadcast in 1978 included Marques' father, Manu, then an All-American defensive lineman at UCLA. That last name seemed a whole lot harder to pronounce back then!

As for the coaches, I'll always be indebted to Don James and to Jim Lambright for educating me on the finer points of the game. I'll never be at their level of football sophistication, but I regard both men as mentors in my development.

Those are just some of the memories I have of calling games at Husky Stadium. It's been the experience of a lifetime to be associated with this program. People take great pride in Husky football, and it's touching so many of them have come to associate me with Washington athletics. I can't tell you how many times someone has yelled "Touchdown, Washington" to me.

Everyone says it's my "signature call," but it's not really anything I ever intended as a trademark. It was just a natural enough thing to say: the team scored, and it was "Touchdown, Washington." Whatever inflection or tone I gave it just got people's attention over the years. If that's a signature, I can't think of a better one.

I also believe the fans' perception of their radio broadcaster is influenced by the fortunes of the team. The better the team, maybe the better the play-by-play guy. I think that's just human nature and, again, it's been a really fortunate circumstance for me. I've been with this team during its glory days, at least in the modern era. We have witnessed the Huskies in absolutely their finest hours.

There's one more reason Husky Stadium is such a special place to me. In the summer of 1997, my wife Molly and I were married there...right on the 50-yard line. Mike Rohrbach, the Husky team chaplain and former Rose Bowl linebacker, performed the ceremony. It was the sort of postcard day that makes Husky Stadium the one-of-a-kind setting it is: land meeting water, blues meeting greens, and, of course, purple meeting gold. Just as the players do, Molly and I walked out of the tunnel and onto the stadium floor, rooflines looming above, family and friends gathered below. "Touchdown, Washington" never felt so good!

From such things does character develop. We become part of the character of Husky Stadium. And it becomes part of us.

Go Dawgs!

HUSKY S T A D I U M

A Field of Greatness

Soaring with cathedral grandeur from the shore of Lake Washington upward through rows of stands to the sweep of twin cantilevered roofs 16 stories above an emerald field, Husky Stadium presents one of the most imposing football venues in the nation. Looming quiet in the morning mist that shrouds it or shot through with light that glances from gold helmets in the wild-cheering frenzy of a Saturday afternoon, it has, for more than 80 years, granted players and fans some of life's sweetest, most exhilarating and most unforgettable moments.

With Lake Washington's Union Bay and the snow-capped Cascade Mountains as a backdrop, Husky Stadium occupies one of college football's most scenic locations. But, it is more than 100 yards of attractive gridiron real estate in picture-postcard country. The stadium has been the setting for classic games, legendary individual achievements and unique traditions that grace the annals of college football.

Beyond that, it has served as a monumental outdoor stage for dramatically depicting the rich heritage and robust growth of the University of Washington and the Pacific Northwest.

When the structure was first planned in 1920, a University of Washington student publication declared: "The Stadium will rear above the surroundings as a monument of imposing dignity." Prophetically, the lofty expectation has been met.

Yet, the origins of Husky football and its glorious stadium are humble, as might be expected of a game imported to the West. The early history of the Washington football program — for the 30 years before the construction of Husky Stadium — was a nomadic journey through a variety of Seattle-area parks and

fields. Those first teams, however, attracted the attention of the region's citizens at the very time the city began a remarkable transformation from a small logging community to a diversified metropolis.

Originally founded as Territorial University in September 1861, the University of

The migration of the sport of football to the Pacific Northwest was inadvertently sparked by the great Seattle fire of June 1889. After the blaze leveled 25 city blocks comprising some 60 acres of waterfront property south of University Street, stories heralding the rebuilding of Seattle and its "boom town" nature

the sport's rulebook. The game was held Thanksgiving Day, November 28, 1889, at Jackson Street Baseball Park. The field was located south of Jackson Street in a large, open area bounded by 16th Avenue on the west and Florence on the east. The game was not sanctioned by the University and was generally

"The Stadium will rear above the surroundings as a monument of imposing dignity."

Washington opened for classes on November 4 on a knoll overlooking Elliott Bay in downtown Seattle. The first public university on the West Coast, it had few students and no athletic field. Asa Mercer, the school's first president and only instructor, taught in the school's main building, a stately, two-story structure. Territorial University became the University of Washington in November 1889, when the region gained statehood. That same year the school fielded its first football team.

began circulating through the country. Tales of frontier life lured fortune hunters and adventurers, including recent graduates from eastern colleges. Some of these hearty souls had played football during their collegiate careers.

Accounts of Washington's first game describe it as a match-up of the Eastern College Alumni and a team of University of Washington students who, under the direction of a student named Frank Griffith, raised enough money to send to Philadelphia for a football and a copy of

frowned upon by its administration.

In lieu of uniforms, which they didn't have, Washington players wore woolen undershirts and baggy pants made of tent canvas. Helmets had not yet been introduced to the sport. After the game, which the Alumni won 20-0, the newspaper failed to report that Washington might have fared better if Griffith, Washington's captain, had played the entire game. Unfortunately, he departed with 15 minutes left, a sartorial wreck, with nothing to wear. An

Eastern brute had torn his clothes completely off.

The following year the school scheduled a single game, again on Thanksgiving, and this time in Tacoma. While the team did not score, the result was an improvement as Washington battled the College of Tacoma to a scoreless tie. With no victories, and no points, in two years, the University curtailed football when only eight men turned out for practice in 1891.

At the same time momentum was building for a greater venue for all university activities: a new campus. Leading the effort to relocate the school was Edmund Meany. One of the first University of Washington graduates, he sponsored a bill in the Washington legislature that authorized the purchase of 580 acres of land at what was known as the Interlaken site: an area between Lake Union and Lake Washington. The total cost of the land was $28,313.75, backed by a $150,000 construction appropriation.

As the campus population grew, student organizations emerged including the Athletic Association, which would later be renamed the Associated Students of the

Opposite: Territorial University of Washington was the first public university on the West Coast when founded in September 1861. Classes were first held in this building on Denny Knoll in downtown Seattle.

Edmund Meany led establishment of the University's new campus. He later joined the faculty and played a key role in major school developments. Above, he addresses the crowd at Washington Stadium.

HUSKY STADIUM

Ralph Nichols (inset) was Washington's first gridiron star. He was a starting guard for three season beginning in 1892. Nichols was the 1894 team captain and served as coach in 1895, 1896 and 1898. Washington's 1893 football team was the first to face a collegiate opponent, losing to Stanford in the season finale.

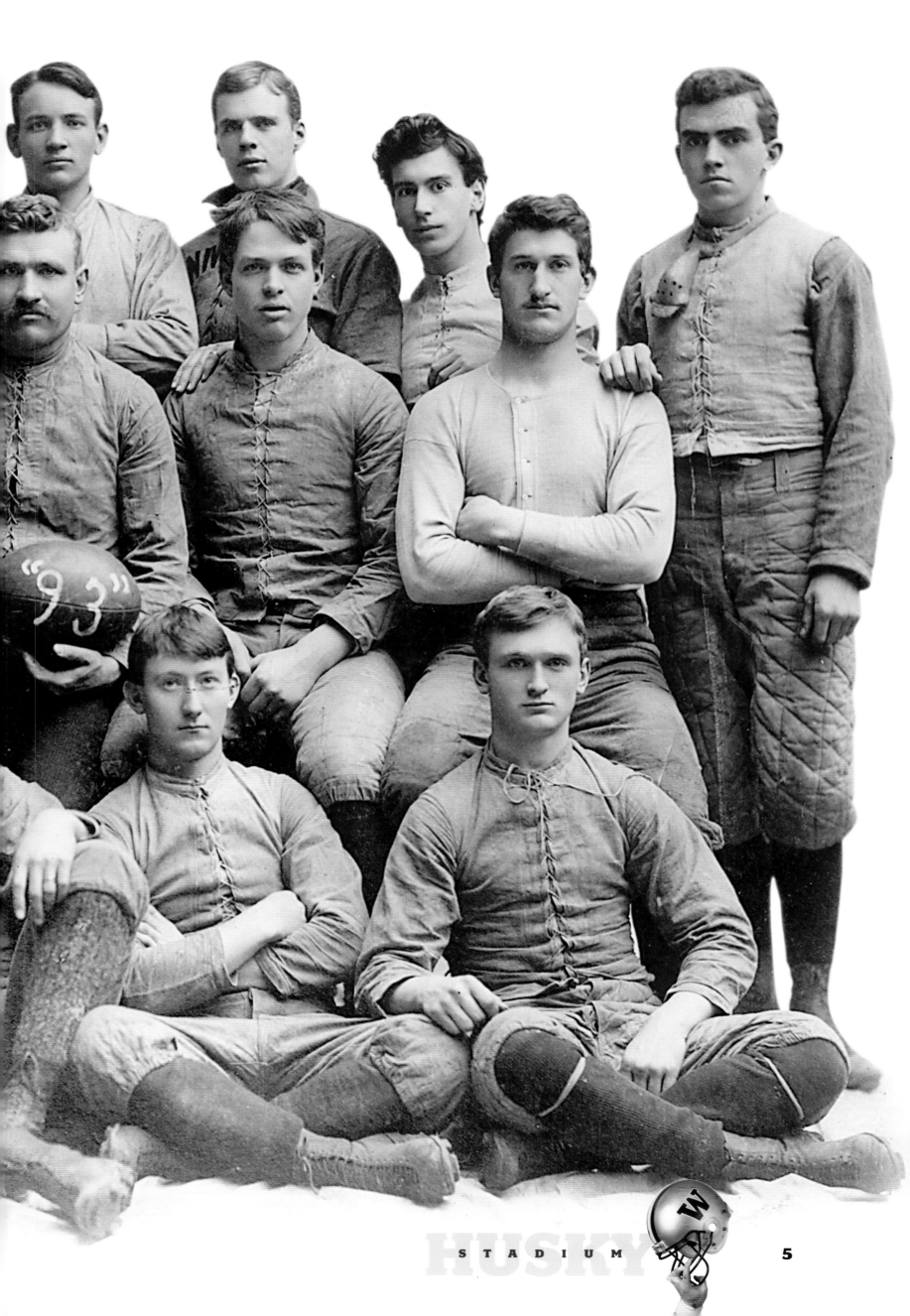

University of Washington (ASUW). In an effort to emulate the traditions of more established college athletic programs, a student assembly was called in 1892 to adopt school colors. Factions debated to a stalemate the use of the nation's colors, red, white and blue, as school colors in honor of George Washington, the University's namesake. Some regarded the choice as a patriotic tribute; others considered it an inappropriate gesture.

The discussion ended when a young English instructor, Miss Louise Frazyer, stood and recited from the first stanza of Lord Byron's "Destruction of Sennacherib" these lines:

The Assyrian came down like a wolf on the fold,
And his cohorts were gleaming in purple and gold;
And the sheen of their spears was like stars on the sea,
When the blue wave rolls nightly on deep Galilee.

The students quickly agreed: purple and gold, the colors of royalty, would become the first great tradition of Washington athletics, and one that has stood the test of time.

Washington named its first coach, William "Billy" Goodwin, for the two-game 1892 season. After losing to Seattle Athletic Club in mid-October, Goodwin's gridders

While equipment for college football teams at the turn of the century was bare bones, some players wore protective nose guards like those seen on Washington's 1895 squad. The team posted a 4-0-1 record for the first undefeated season in school history.

won the rematch on December 17 at the Madison Street Athletic Park, claiming the school's first victory. Fullback Frank Atkins, who had played in Washington's first game as a pre-collegiate student, ran five yards for the school's first touchdown in the 14-0 win. To celebrate the victory, students paraded through downtown streets. At the offices of the *Seattle Post-Intelligencer*, the University lads gave three cheers as the score was chalked on a large bulletin board.

Washington played five games in 1893, including its first intercollegiate contest.

Stanford visited on December 29 and won 40-0 before 600 spectators in West Seattle. The Stanford travel party included a manager named Herbert Hoover, who would become the nation's 31st President (1929-33).

In 1895, when the new University campus became a reality, the football team found an on-campus practice site at University Athletic Field on the north end of campus, while playing games at a variety of off-campus locations. The practice field paid immediate dividends as Washington enjoyed its first unbeaten season, outscoring opponents 98-8 in com-

piling a 4-0-1 record.

With only a handful of West Coast colleges fielding teams and with funds for travel to out-of-town schools limited, Washington's first decade of football was played primarily against Seattle athletic clubs, YMCA teams and small local colleges. That began changing in 1900 when Idaho, Washington State and Oregon first appeared on the schedule. Two years later,

Left: The 1894 team recorded Washington's first shutout victory, a 46-0 defeat of Whitman, and claimed the state championship. Right: When the campus moved to its current location in 1895, the Administration Building, later renamed Denny Hall, was the central structure of the new academic community.

The 1896 team poses with its City Championship trophy after defeating the teams of Seattle YMCA and Seattle Athletic Club. University Field (below), later renamed Denny Field, as it appeared on the new campus in the early 1900s. Lewis and Clark Halls are to the southeast.

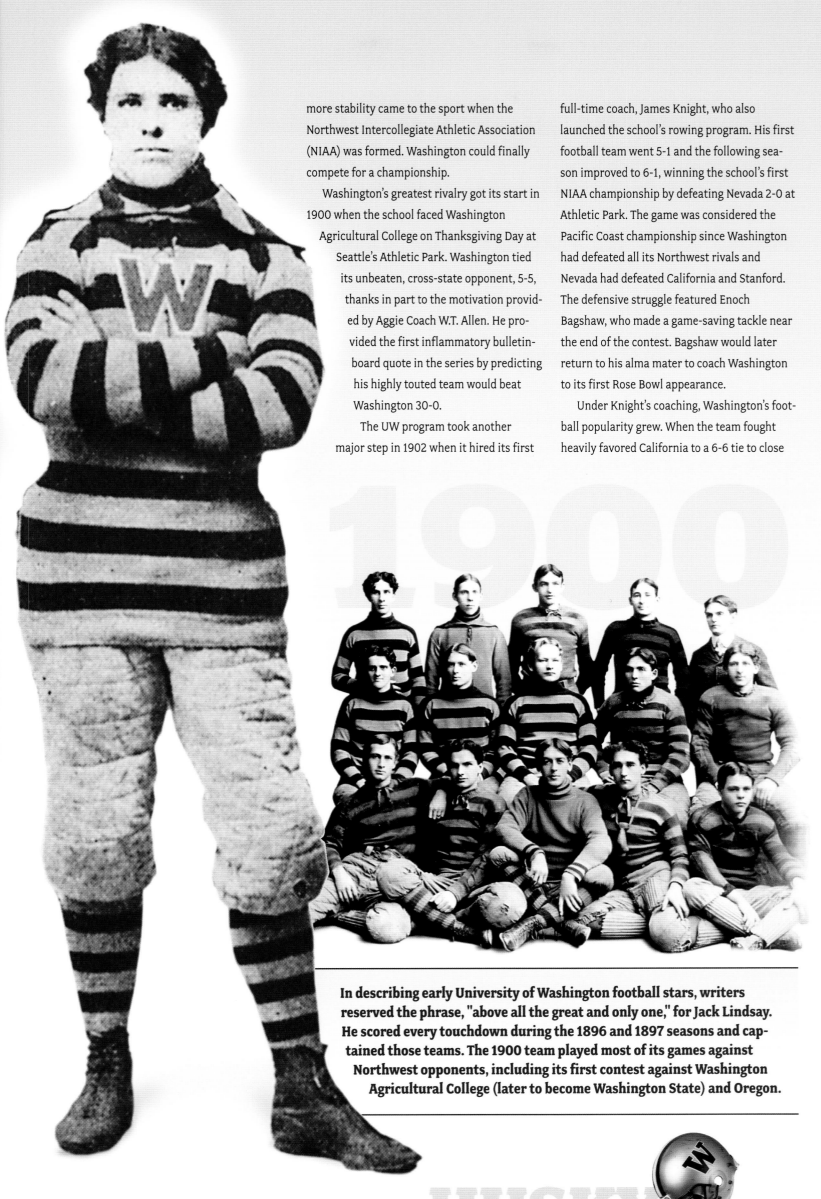

more stability came to the sport when the Northwest Intercollegiate Athletic Association (NIAA) was formed. Washington could finally compete for a championship.

Washington's greatest rivalry got its start in 1900 when the school faced Washington Agricultural College on Thanksgiving Day at Seattle's Athletic Park. Washington tied its unbeaten, cross-state opponent, 5-5, thanks in part to the motivation provided by Aggie Coach W.T. Allen. He provided the first inflammatory bulletin-board quote in the series by predicting his highly touted team would beat Washington 30-0.

The UW program took another major step in 1902 when it hired its first full-time coach, James Knight, who also launched the school's rowing program. His first football team went 5-1 and the following season improved to 6-1, winning the school's first NIAA championship by defeating Nevada 2-0 at Athletic Park. The game was considered the Pacific Coast championship since Washington had defeated all its Northwest rivals and Nevada had defeated California and Stanford. The defensive struggle featured Enoch Bagshaw, who made a game-saving tackle near the end of the contest. Bagshaw would later return to his alma mater to coach Washington to its first Rose Bowl appearance.

Under Knight's coaching, Washington's football popularity grew. When the team fought heavily favored California to a 6-6 tie to close

In describing early University of Washington football stars, writers reserved the phrase, "above all the great and only one," for Jack Lindsay. He scored every touchdown during the 1896 and 1897 seasons and captained those teams. The 1900 team played most of its games against Northwest opponents, including its first contest against Washington Agricultural College (later to become Washington State) and Oregon.

"And in the nights of winter,
    When cold the north winds blow,
And the dripping of the eaves
    Is heard amidst the snow
With cheering and with laughter
    Will the story then be told,
How well Washington won the game
    In the College days of old."

In the first meeting between Washington and cross-state rival Washington State (Washington Agricultural College at the time), the teams fought to a 5-5 draw on a muddy field on Thanksgiving Day 1900 at Seattle's Athletic Park. On November 21, 1901, Washington beat Idaho 10-0. The 1903 Tyee included a poem to the loyal Purple and Gold defenders.

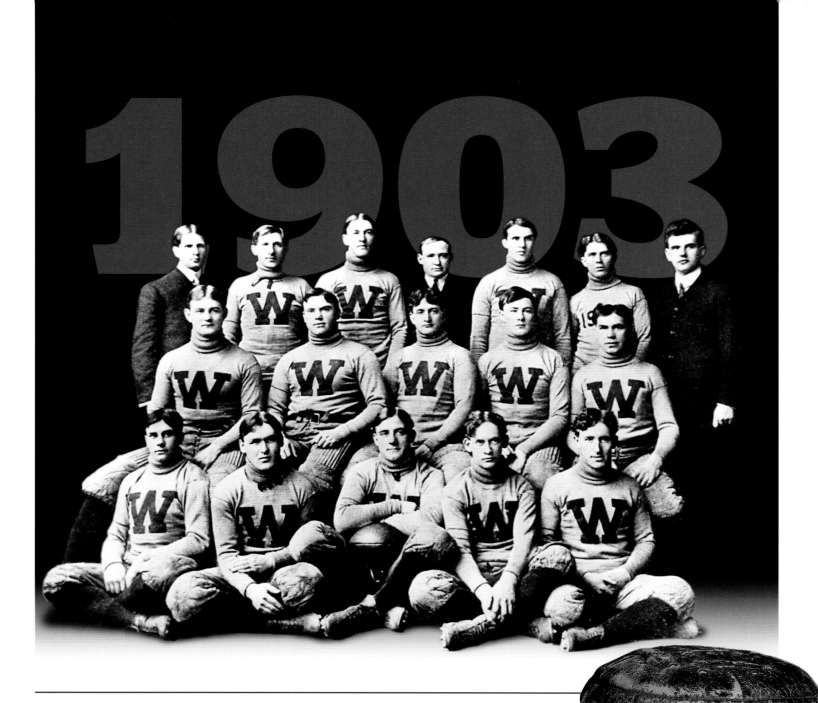

1903

In 1903 Washington was crowned Pacific Coast champion with a 6-1-0 record. In the early days of football, some players protected their noses and mouths with metal nose guards (right) suspended from the front of their helmets. Chief Joseph, the famous Nez Perce leader, made his first visit to Seattle in 1903 and attended the Washington-Nevada game.

the 1904 season, a crowd of 3,000 cheered their hometown heroes. In April 1906, the ASUW recommended that bleachers be erected at University Athletic Field (later renamed Denny Field) to encourage holding athletic events on campus rather than in the city.

On October 26, 1906, the eve of the team's first on-campus game, *The Pacific Wave*, the student weekly newspaper, reported that every carpenter available had helped complete covered grandstands with seating for 1,200 people, all sheltered from the rain and sleet by a roof of "good and fat boards." The newspaper also noted: "For the benefit of the players, it would be best to add that little

stones which are now so much in evidence on the field will be removed, so there will be no danger of one of the contestants falling thereon and thereby breeding a scab on the end of the nose or marring his beauty in any manner."

In its home debut, Washington tied Oregon
continued on page 15

When Washington and Idaho battled to a scoreless tie in 1907, the outcome appeared meaningless. But it marked the start of Washington's 63-game unbeaten streak that remains an NCAA record.

"No smile, no handshakes, no slap on the back... nothing but a pair of eyes peering coldly out of a dark face..."

—A player's description of meeting new coach Gil Dobie in 1908.

(Above) Gil Dobie's dour demeanor earned him the nickname "Gloomy Gil," but his psychological ploys and insistence on perfection worked. Washington never lost a game during his nine seasons as head coach. The 1908 team, Gil Dobie's first at Washington, shutout four opponents and allowed a total of only 15 points during a seven-game schedule. Denny Field (top right) was the first stadium site on the new campus. Initially used for practices and scrimmages, it was eventually fenced and flanked by covered, wood-frame bleachers along the north and south sidelines.

Agricultural 0-0. The new surroundings proved unproductive for Washington as well as for opponents, as the next two games at University Athletic Field also resulted in scoreless ties. It was not until the final game of the 1906 season, a 16-9 victory against Idaho, that Washington finally scored at home. Ironically, a scoreless tie a year later against Idaho at University Athletic Field would mark the start of one of the greatest streaks in the history of college football.

When Gil Dobie arrived on the Washington campus in 1908, he hardly presented the appearance of a football coach. The tall, lanky Scotsman let his demeanor speak for him. A group of entering freshmen was among the first to meet the new coach and, as one of them recalled: "No smile, no handshakes, no slap on the back ... nothing but a pair of eyes peering coldly out of a dark face that was hidden partially by a slouch hat drawn loosely over a head of mussed black hair."

After a brief introduction, Dobie, in a rasping voice, stated: "Remember, all you fellows, practice Monday starts at 2 p.m. One thing I demand is promptness." His concern for promptness, his preparation for games, and his psychological skills paid off handsomely. During his nine years at Washington, Dobie's

continued on page 18

"The Assyrian came down
like a wolf on the fold,
And his cohorts were gleaming
in purple
and gold;
And the sheen of their spears
was like stars on the sea,
When the blue wave rolls nightly
on deep Galilee."

— from Lord Byron's "Destruction of Sennacherib"

HUSKY

S T A D I U M

17

teams never lost a game, winning 58 times and playing to a tie on three occasions. Dobie's players outscored opponents by a remarkably lopsided 1,930 to 118 margin. From 1907 to 1917 Washington's teams built an incredible streak of 63 games without a defeat. The achievement, that includes a tie with Idaho in 1907, remains an NCAA record for consecutive games without a loss.

In the midst of the football program's successes, one of Washington's greatest traditions was born. In 1915, Lester J. Wilson, a 1913 UW graduate, wrote words and music for "Bow Down

to Washington," the school's "Prize Song." His original lyrics included a second chorus intended solely for the California game. It declared, in part: "See the Golden Bear, From his mighty lair, For we're goin' to hang his carcass in the Northland."

Dobie's teams were loaded with players who were Washington's first stars. Huber "Polly" Grimm started for the 1905, 1907, 1909 and 1910 teams as a tackle, placekicker and punter. He was a captain during his final season and was the first Washington player to receive national honors when he was chosen a third-team All-American by Walter Camp. Quarterback and field general William "Wee" Coyle led the team to four undefeated seasons from 1908 to 1911. Louis Seagrave became Washington's first first-team All-American. He was selected as a guard on Walter Camp's Football

Below: Washington's Mel Mucklestone breaks clear while quarterback Wee Coyle, on the far left, trails the play in the 20-6 victory over Oregon in 1909 that gave Washington its first perfect season. Guy Flaherty (left) is the namesake for Washington's most esteemed individual football award, which goes to the Husky player voted "most inspirational" by teammates. In 1908, Flaherty was the award's first recipient. Top right: Washington's defense stops an Oregon running back in a 10-0 win against Oregon in 1914. Right: 1910-era leather pennant.

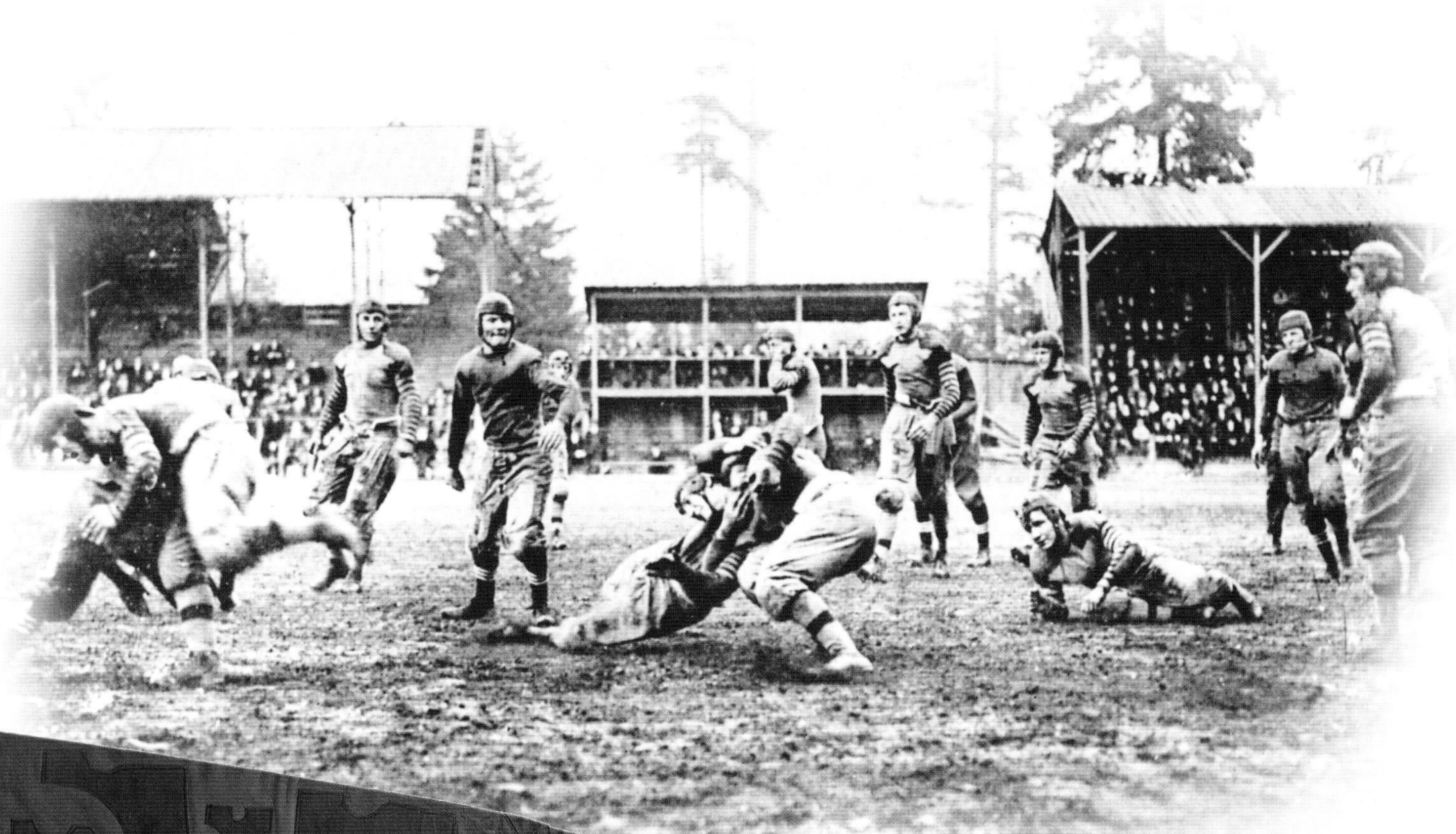

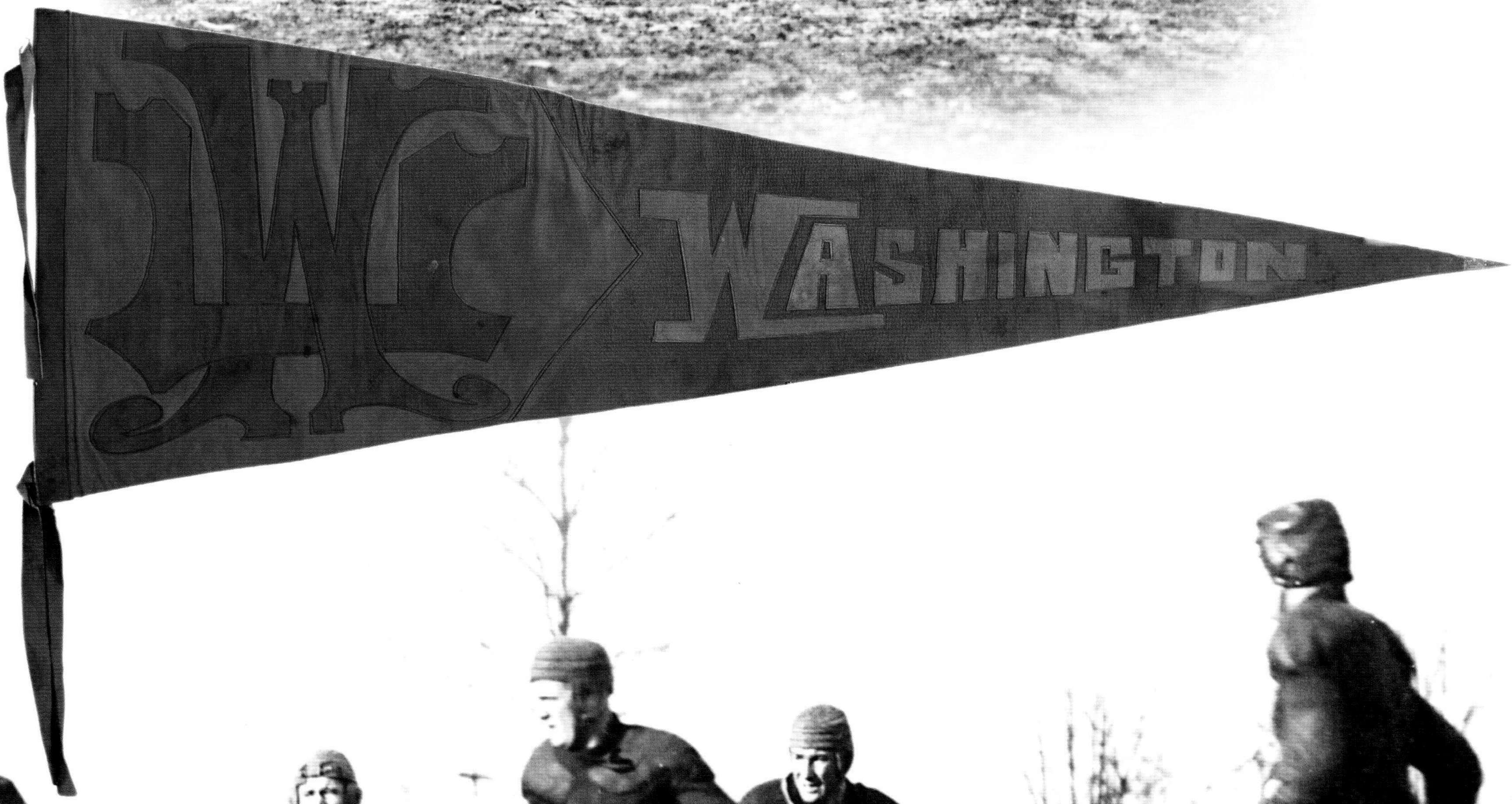
W
WASHINGTON

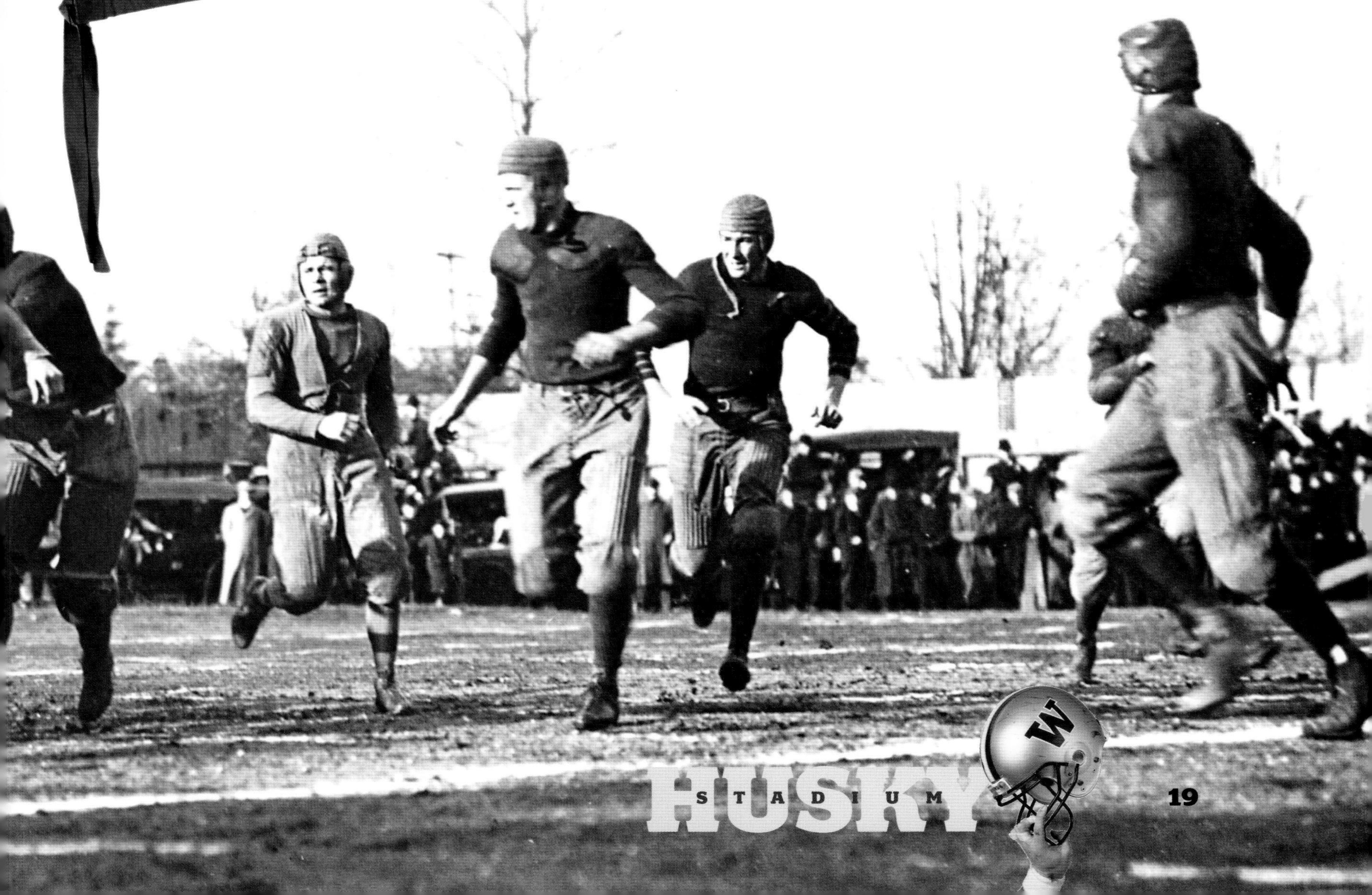

FIGHT SONG

Foundation team in 1916. He played on four unbeaten teams (1913-1916) and was the captain of Dobie's last Washington team in 1916.

Toward the end of Dobie's amazing run at Washington, the Pacific Coast Conference (PCC), predecessor to the Pac-8 and later the Pac-10, was formed. In 1916, Dobie's last season

Bow Down to Washington,
Bow Down to Washington,
Mighty Are the Men
Who Wear the Purple and the Gold,
Joyfully We Welcome Them
Within the Victors' Fold.
We Will Carve Their Names
In the Hall of Fame
To Preserve the Memory of Our Devotion.
Heaven Help the Foes of Washington;
They're Trembling at the Feet
Of Mighty Washington,
The Boys Are There With Bells,
Their Fighting Blood Excels,
It's Harder to Push Them Over the Line
Than Pass the Dardanelles.
Victory 's the Cry of Washington...
Leather Lungs Together
With a Rah! Rah! Rah!
And O'er the Land
Our Loyal Band
Will Sing the Glory
Of Washington Forever.

Bill Horsley (top left), yell leader in 1911, created and designed the Hook. At the time the expression, "Get the Hook," was popular. Above: Horsley leads the fans in a serpentine on Denny Field at the 1911 Thanksgiving Day game. Knights of the Hook, gathered around their symbol, lead Washington rooters at half time on Denny Field. Below: This "broomstick" down marker kept teams, fans and officials on track at Denny Field.

in Seattle, Washington won the inaugural PCC championship. The final game of the season proved to be another milestone for the growing program. More than 9,000 fans jammed Denny Field to watch Washington beat California 14-7. It was the largest crowd to ever see the team play.

Despite the championship, the season ended on a sour note when Dobie decided to leave Washington. He lost the backing of the faculty when he sided with a player in a dispute over an academic suspension. While never duplicating his phenomenal Washington streak of victories, Dobie went on to successfully coach at Navy, Cornell and Boston College. He finished his coaching career in 1938 with a record of 180-45-15 and an illustrious .784 winning percentage.

Surprisingly, Dobie's teams never received a bowl game invitation. In 1916, Washington State was selected to face Brown in the Rose Bowl on the basis of comparative scores. A year later Oregon was presented the invitation because railroad fare from Eugene to Pasadena for the entire team was $250 cheaper than from Seattle.

Thanks to the success of the Washington program, however, Denny Field underwent several upgrades to

Above: William "Wee" Coyle was quarterback of four undefeated teams from 1908 to 1911. Coach Dobie claimed Coyle never made a mistake as his signal caller. Huber "Polly" Grimm (standing at left) was the first Washington football player to receive national honors. He starred on the 1905, 1907, 1909 and 1910 teams as tackle, place-kicker, punter and runner in the tackle-around-play. On occasion, he was a passer and pass receiver. He was also the AAU heavyweight wrestling champion in 1911. In 1916, Louis Seagrave (kneeling) became Washington's first All-American.

accommodate the growing crowds. A large grandstand was built on the south side of the field in 1911. Five years later the area was re-graded and a larger north grandstand was added to increase capacity.

The first nickname for Washington's athletic teams was adopted in November 1919. As a protest to the banning of the popular campus

magazine, *Sun Dodger*, students applied the name to school teams. As a negative reference to the Northwest's climate, however, Sun Dodgers was deemed less than inspiring, and in 1921 a student committee was formed to find a more suitable moniker. Frustrated by the committee's progress, athletic officials, acting while students were away on a holiday break in December 1921, decided to refer to Washington teams as Vikings. Students protested the choice and, within two months, settled on Huskies — a name considered appropriate because of the University's proximity to the Alaskan frontier.

In 1919, a crowd of 16,000 watched Washington stun highly regarded California 7-0 at Denny Field. While the record crowd cheered wildly, thousands of other fans were turned away at the gates for lack of seating. It was clear that a larger facility was needed.

The move to replace Denny Field began in November 1919 when Darwin Meisnest, the 24-year-old graduate manager of the ASUW student organization, proposed a new stadium at the first student assembly of the year. When Meisnest took his post earlier in the year, two large projects were before the ASUW: a

With its large covered-seating sections, Denny Field enabled fans to dodge the elements during games. Top: Denny Field was standing-room-only for the California game in 1916. Washington won 14-7 to capture the first football championship of the newly-formed Pacific Coast Conference. It was the last game Dobie coached at Washington. Darwin Meisnest (inset above), the ASUW graduate manager, proposed a new stadium and started the fund-raising effort.

new athletic stadium and a new student union. He persuaded students that a stadium, not a student union, should be built first because it would receive the financial support of the business community while the student union would not.

Meisnest was right. Most of the $260,000 raised prior to completion resulted from the sale of 3,500 plaques, many of them to enthusiastic businesses. Within a year, Washington students were able to contribute $100,000 toward the stadium's construction. University President Henry Suzzallo and the Board of Regents quickly approved the ASUW's recommendation, and a Stadium Committee was

established. Its members engaged University architects C. H. Bebe and Carl F. Gould for the project. Appointed in early March, Bebe and Gould boldly promised that "the stadium can be built by November 27, if the work is unhampered by industrial difficulties."

Gould and University engineering professor Charles May, a former Washington player, gathered ideas by touring stadiums at Yale, Princeton, Cornell, Michigan and Tacoma. Based on their survey, plans were prepared to orient the stadium to Lake Washington, the forested hills beyond, and the Cascade Mountains in the distance. The University's Astronomy Department was asked to establish the stadium's longitudinal axis to "avoid as far as possible the glare of the sun in the stadium for the benefit of the players." Based on astronomical measurements, its axis was set approximately at right angle to the sun's rays — at 71 degrees, 50 minutes west of north.

The Committee recommended a stadium with an ultimate seating capacity of 60,000, built in two phases of 30,000 seats each. The

Above: Football used in last Thanksgiving Day game on Denny Field, in 1919. Washington defeated California 7-0. Right: Original plans for the new stadium called for seating capacity of 60,000, with two great towers surmounting the main entrance at the west end. Only the lower section, however, with 30,000 seats, was initially completed. Nonetheless, the amount raised for the stadium project was remarkable for the time.

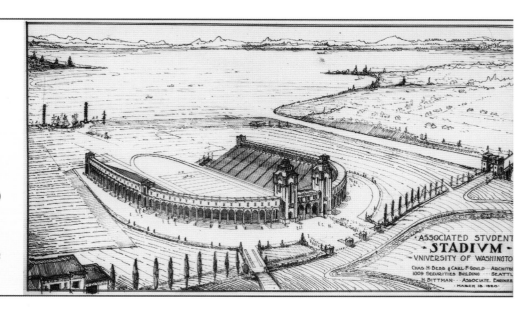

HUSKY STADIUM   **23**

structure would be an open-ended bowl to preserve the site's scenic views of the lake and mountains to the east. Though never completed, the design called for two great Collegiate Gothic towers surmounting the main entrance on the west. Four smaller towers were planned, two each on the north and south sides of the stadium. A colonnade would provide space for memorials, inscription of records and a covered practice track. The field would be encircled by a full quarter-mile track with a 220-yard straight-away on the north side.

A statewide fund-raising campaign, launched in the spring of 1920, was supported by the Washington State Chamber of Commerce, its affiliated commercial bodies and the alumni and students of the University. Loyal Washingtonians visited virtually every firm in Seattle seeking contributions. Five-hundred student salespersons sold small bronze plaques to supporters who bought season tickets. The price of a plaque was $50 for two years and $100 for five years, reduced to $25 and $50 for purchasers living more than 50 miles from the city. Plaque sales eventually resulted in more than $240,000 for stadium construction.

Students aided the cause by approving an ASUW recommendation to raise student fees from $5 to $10 and allocate $4 of the fee to pay a portion of the initial stadium costs and help retire bonds issued to pay the contractor's fee. The fees provided almost $124,000 for construction.

The stadium's groundbreaking ceremony was held April 16, 1920. University President Suzzallo and Seattle Mayor Hugh Campbell were joined by students, faculty and prominent stadium supporters. Three weeks later Puget Sound Bridge and Dredging Company signed a contract with the ASUW and work began.

The entire excavation of the field and the filling of the side embankments was accomplished with hydraulic sluices and pumps. Great pressurized streams of water — 687-million gallons taken from the nearby lakes — gouged the earth and washed it away into directed channels. In this way, 230,000-cubic-yards of dirt and silt were removed, leaving a

Left: Bronze plaques bought by Washington supporters resulted in more than $240,000 for stadium construction. Below: Seattle Mayor Hugh Campbell (left) and University President Henry Suzzallo break ground for the new stadium on April 16, 1920.

drainable base of sand and gravel.

Four-thousand barrels of concrete, poured on this base and reinforced by 106 tons of steel, formed the foundation for the stadium seats.

As the bowl took shape, 100,000-feet of Douglas fir lumber were used to build 30 rows of benches, laid out in 32 sections. The seating pattern and aisles enabled the original capacity crowd of 30,000 to exit the stadium in seven minutes. To handle wet weather conditions that were sure to plague the field, 8,000 cubic yards of drainage gravel were laid over and around 6,500 feet of four-inch drainage tiles placed every 25 feet along the length of the football field.

Finally, 3,500-cubic-yards of topsoil were hauled to the site to create the gridiron surface. Approximately 2,000-cubic-yards of cinder were spread on the running track. In the two weeks before the stadium opened, a little, steam-driven tandem roller traveled 180 miles up and down the field in one-yard strips to make it level and firm. A "sunken passage" was built to separate fans from the field while providing drainage. It was calculated that for every inch of rain that fell on the structural portion of the stadium, 36,000 gallons of water would accumulate.

The project was completed in little more than a year from the time of Meisnest's proposal.

Meanwhile, the Huskies played their first four home games of the 1920 season at Denny Field. A crowd of 9,000 attended the final game that saw Stanford defeat Washington 3-0. Washington played its last game at Denny Field like its first — unable to score a point.

A series of events to celebrate the opening of the new stadium was held involving students, alumni, politicians, the business community and fans. Seattle Mayor Campbell declared a citywide holiday to encourage citizens to attend the game with Dartmouth. Homecoming festivities began on Wednesday, November 24, when the University Glee Club and Jazz

Top: This photo, taken about a month before the opening game, shows seats installed on the north side of the stadium. Middle: A view taken on November 13, 1920 shows the completion of seating on the west and south sides. Bottom: On November 20th, one week before the opening game on November 27, 1920, the field was almost complete.

Band held a concert at Meany Hall. The next day, players for Broadway and Lincoln high schools met on Denny Field for the traditional Thanksgiving Day inter-city football game. Friday's events included an auto parade in downtown Seattle, a huge pep rally and bonfire at Denny Field and a "College Night" that included alumni from more than 70 schools.

The student newspaper, *University of Washington Daily*, reported: "The spirit shown by the turnout, in the face of the weather conditions, and the volume which the gathering was able to put into its cheers, convinced even the most pessimistic of supporters that Dartmouth will have to fight not only the Washington team, but the Washington student body, when it takes the field against the Purple and Gold football eleven."

Fans came from all directions. They traveled on foot and by automobile, bus and trolley. A small number even arrived by boat. Those coming by auto from the south drove over University Bridge and Fremont Bridge, both constructed as part of the Lake Washington Ship Canal project. Since Montlake Bridge was not completed until 1925, a pontoon bridge spanned Montlake Canal for the sake of pedestrians coming from neighborhoods south of the canal.

Pre-game ceremonies included an appearance by Washington Governor Louis Hart and a 17-gun military salute. A detachment of U.S.

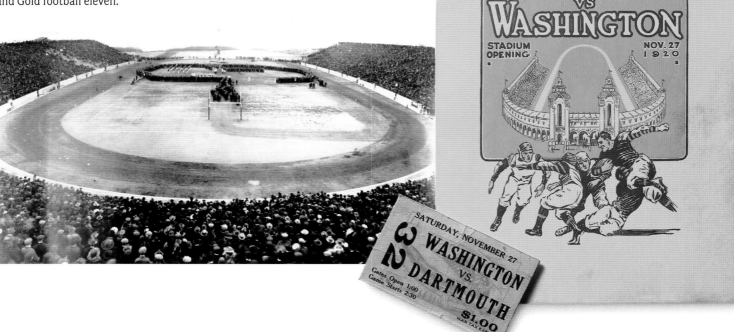

Marines raised the American flag to the accompaniment of "To the Colors." The Knights of the Hook, the school's first pep group, paraded and led the student section in choruses of yells. In the women's rooting section, a big purple and gold "W" was formed.

To the cheers of 24,500 fans, the two teams emerged from a tunnel on the south side of the stadium: first the Dartmouth squad, with a 6-2 record, followed by the 1-4 Washington team. The match-up marked the first inter-sectional game for Washington. Bob Abel, Washington's quarterback and the ASUW president, scored the first touchdown in the new stadium on the game's opening drive. When Dartmouth attempted a field goal, Abel broke through the line and blocked the kick. The ball bounced into his hands, and he rambled 63 yards for the historic score. Abel's return, however, would be the only highlight for Washington. Sporting a solid passing game, Dartmouth scored four times to defeat Washington 28-7.

A contest to name the field had been conducted before the stadium was completed. Approximately 2,500 names were entered, of which all but about 400 were duplications. Some were of a humorous nature: "Washington Dimple," "Wash Bowl," "Tub" and "Basin." The finalists were "Crater," "Cascadium," and "Washington Field." The last one, submitted by Harold Sheerer, plant engineer of the Seattle Shipping Board, was declared the winner. He received $100 and immediately bought a seat plaque with his winnings. The name remained Washington Field until the late 1960s when the term Husky Stadium came into popular use.

Washington's stadium, considered an engineering marvel because of its quick construction schedule and attention to detail, inspired similar models at Stanford in 1921 and at the Los Angeles Coliseum and California-Berkeley in 1923.

The new stadium also introduced traffic jams to the city. The site had been isolated by Montlake Cut, which opened in 1917 in the final phase of the Lake Washington Ship Canal project. University Bridge, opened in 1919, was

Cars parked east of Montlake Boulevard at a game in the early 1920s. Fans coming to the new stadium created traffic jams before Montlake Bridge was completed in 1925. Below: Yell leaders in 1920.

the only direct route to the stadium for most of Seattle's population. At the time the ship canal was completed, three of four piers for Montlake Bridge were in place, but the fourth was unfinished for lack of city funds. The

continued on page 30

"You had to run between the rocks. You could practically hide behind them."

— All-American running back Chuck Carroll on the playing surface of Washington Field in 1928.

bring their boats to the contests and tie up along the stadium's shoreline. In years to come, more and more water craft would join this mode of transportation, adding a special quality to the pageantry of game day.

While built principally to serve as home for Washington football, Washington Field possessed an availability and capacity that made it an attractive location for a wide range of impressive outdoor productions. During the early years, revenue from non-football events at the stadium helped retire bonds issued to finance its construction.

Among the most financially and artistically successful of these events was a series of grand pageants. The first of the productions, staged at the open east end of the stadium, was a nationally famous religious spectacle, *The Wayfarer*. It appeared at Washington Field from July 23 to 30, 1921. Written by a former Seattle minister,

Reverend J. E. Crowther, *The Wayfarer* was a combination of grand opera, oratorio, pageantry and drama presented on an enormous scale. Over 88,000 people attended performances. It proved so successful that it was presented again in 1922 and 1925, with more than 150,000 witnessing the production in those two years.

opening of the stadium forced city officials to complete the span, and a bond issue was passed. Montlake Bridge finally opened in 1925 and, coupled with the growing popularity of automobiles, played a significant role in the city's northward expansion.

The opening of Montlake Cut and the traffic issues associated with attending games at the new stadium led some enterprising fans to

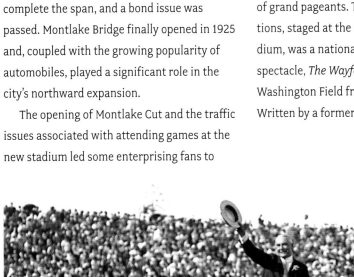

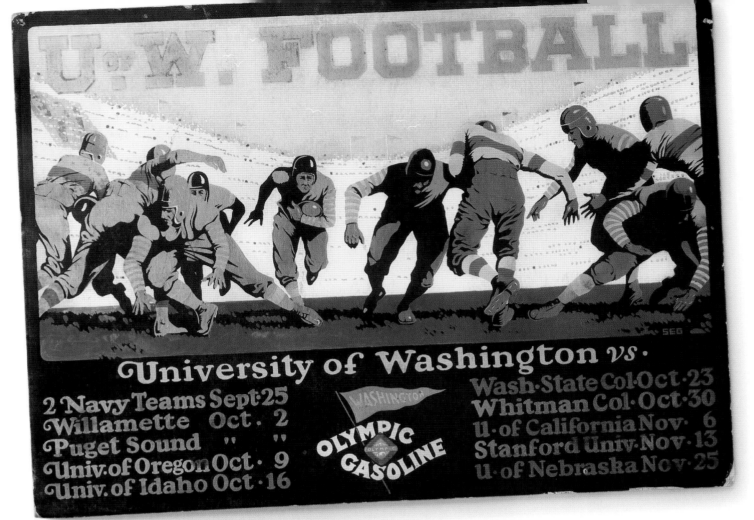

Washington history professor Edmund Meany, along with Montgomery Lynch, penned a patriotic pageant that was staged on Washington Field in 1923. *Americanus* boasted a cast of 10,000, the largest ever assembled for a staged event of its kind in the country. More than 42,000 tickets were sold for the performance.

Americanus was one of several major events held in Seattle in late July of 1923 to coincide with the city's Merchant's Exposition. The highlight of festivities came on July 27 when President Warren Harding arrived as part of a 22-day transcontinental presidential trip. Speaking mid-afternoon at the stadium before a crowd of 40,000, he recounted his observations of the Territory of Alaska and his interest in its becoming a state. It was to be one of Harding's last speeches. He died of an illness in San Francisco six days later.

In its early years, Washington Field also hosted Fourth of July celebrations as well as concerts, dances and other special events. In 1925, 10,000 persons, mostly of Norwegian descent, gathered at the stadium to celebrate the Norse Centennial, marking the 100th anniversary of the first permanent settlement of Norwegians in the U.S.

Five years after the stadium's completion, a final financial report was released at the January 1926 meeting of the ASUW's Board of Control. The report placed the total cost of construction at $565,034.98 and listed the payment sources:

Plaque sales:	$241,102.00
ASUW Building Fund:	123,519.48
Stadium non-football events, including pageants, concerts, and Fourth of July celebrations:	107,100.00
Small donations:	1,400.00
Rose Bowl Game, 1924:	38,000.00
Rose Bowl Game, 1926:	20,000.00
Excess funds from 1925 football budget:	30,000.00
Refund from contractor:	3,913.50
Total payments:	$565,034.98

The last of the bonds to partially finance stadium construction was repaid and symbolically burned during halftime of the 1926 Washington State game, fully eight years before the bonds were scheduled to be retired.

Above: A post card from an early game in Washington Field. Top: 1926 football schedule poster.

While Washington Field was impressive and a valuable resource to the growing Seattle community, it had its drawbacks. "To make the water drain quickly from the field, sand and sawdust were used," said Herman Brix, who starred as a tackle at Washington from 1925-27 and later became a Hollywood star in the role of Tarzan. "As a result the field became very rough and abrasive when it was wet. It was like sandpaper."

"You had to run between the rocks," recalled Chuck Carroll, a consensus All-American at running back in 1928. "You could practically hide behind them. You would get stone bruises, and they would stay with you all season. You always looked forward to playing at Stanford because the Palo Alto stadium had a grass field."

Prior to construction in 1927 of the University of Washington Pavilion (later renamed Clarence S. "Hec" Edmundson Pavilion in 1948 in honor of the legendary Washington basketball coach upon his retirement), Washington players and opponents would dress in the north end of old Lander Hall and enter the stadium through a tunnel beneath the south stands. It was sealed up when new locker rooms and training facilities were opened in the Pavilion. The cutout of the original tunnel can still be seen at the base of section 16 in the stadium.

The new stadium tunnel stretched 362 feet into the Pavilion. Its dirt surface

Chuck Carroll (above) was the second consensus All-American in Husky history. Known as Iron Man for playing almost every minute of every game as a running back and linebacker, he is one of only three Husky football players to have his number, "2", retired. He led the conference in scoring in 1927 and 1928 and was elected to the National Football Foundation Hall of Fame. Top: Chuck Carroll's letter sweater. Right: Hec Edmundson was Washington's legendary basketball and track-and-field coach.

was originally covered with wooden boards. Players said the clatter from their cleats echoing off the concrete walls was deafening. In the days when light bulbs provided illumination, Husky players would smash them as they returned from pre-game warmups, leaving opposing players in the dark as they made their descent down the black passage for the start of the game. Adding a measure of intimidation, Husky players would follow the visitors in the dark tunnel, screaming, cursing, shouting and barking. On more than one occasion, the action started in the tunnel well before the opening coin toss on the field.

UW Daily editor Max Miller, who was on the committee that selected the school's new nickname, and his classmates at Sigma Alpha Epsilon fraternity provided the University its first mascot. They acquired an Alaskan Malamute, named him Frosty, and took him to games and other campus events. He served as school mascot from 1922 to 1929. He was followed by Frosty II from 1930 to 1936, Wasky in 1946, Wasky II in 1947, and Ski, from 1954-1957.

After one season of play in the new stadium, Enoch Bagshaw, a former Washington football captain, joined the program as coach. During nine years at the helm of the team, he helped the Huskies compile a

63-22-6 record.

The stadium did not record its first capacity crowd until 1922 when 30,075 filled Washington Field after the team started the season with five consecutive victories. Purple and Gold patrons left disappointed, however, as California overpowered the Huskies 45-7.

Washington played Southern California for the first time in 1923. The game drew so much interest that the first radio broadcast of a Husky game was arranged. *The Post-Intelligencer's* station KFJC provided "instantaneous radiophone coverage of all the action."

Just sophomores at the time, future Washington stars Elmer Tesreau and George Wilson both scored touchdowns in a 22-0 rout.

"The Huskies swarmed over the touted Trojans like ants on a picnic pie," wrote well-known Seattle sportswriter Royal Brougham. The game was a turning point in rebuilding the Husky program. Washington proceeded to win every game of the season except for a 9-0 loss to California, as the Golden Bears played a final time on their historic California Field.

Despite winning their fourth consecutive PCC title, the Bears declined the 1924 Rose Bowl invitation, and Washington made the trip, tying Navy 14-14 in the University's first bowl appearance.

The Golden Bears, Washington's chief rival at the time, proved the biggest draw. In 1924 over 35,000 fans wedged into Washington Field

Coach Enoch Bagshaw (above) compiled a 63-22-6 record over nine seasons, 1921-1929, and led the Huskies to two Rose Bowls. Left: Frosty, an Alaskan Malamute, was Washington's first live animal mascot. He frolicked on the sidelines from 1922 to 1929. George Wilson (below) was the first consensus All-American in Husky football history. His number, "33", is one of three retired. He was a three-time All-American halfback and member of the 1924 and 1926 Rose Bowl teams. In the 1926 game, he rushed for 134 yards and threw two touchdown passes against Alabama, generating almost all of Washington's offense. He was elected to the College Football Hall of Fame and Rose Bowl Hall of Fame.

to see the Huskies play their northern California rival to a 7-7 draw. A year later, when Bagshaw guided the Huskies to the conference title, another crowd of 35,000 jammed the stadium for UW's showdown with Stanford.

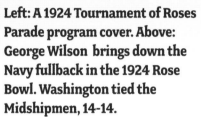

Left: A 1924 Tournament of Roses Parade program cover. Above: George Wilson brings down the Navy fullback in the 1924 Rose Bowl. Washington tied the Midshipmen, 14-14.

GREAT GAMES
W

13 00:00 **00**
WASHINGTON ••• STANFORD

NOVEMBER 7, 1925

Huskies Knock Nevers Dizzy

Coached by the legendary Glen "Pop" Warner, Stanford came north to play Washington in a game that featured two All-American running backs. Stanford boasted captain and powerful fullback Ernie Nevers, while Washington countered with George Wilson, a triple-threat star. The winner of the contest would gain the inside track to the Rose Bowl.

Each squad also featured potent defenses. The lines were evenly matched, both averaging 185 pounds. Washington had surrendered only 16 points in seven previous games. The capacity crowd featured a number of Stanford supporters and more than 8,000 Washington alumni who returned for the game. A new streetcar line conveniently dropped off patrons in front of the stadium turnstiles.

Using a trick play, Washington grabbed the early lead. Wilson was in punt formation, the ends were in the backfield, and Herman Brix lined up as a tackle-eligible receiver. Wilson tossed to Brix for a 20-yard gain. Captain Elmer Tesreau rolled through left tackle to the Stanford 14. After a five-yard loss on an end sweep, Wilson passed to George Guttormsen for the score. Guttormsen's kick was no good and Washington led 6-0. The Huskies threatened one more time before the half ended, but Guttormsen's drop kick from the Stanford 25-yard line was wide.

The play of the Husky defense in the second half was the key to Washington's victory. Facing a fourth-and-two on the Husky 20, Nevers attempted to leap over the center of the Husky line. Tesreau and Wilson suddenly hit him, lifting the Stanford star off the ground and knocking him out. Later, the Cardinal moved the ball to the Washington eight where Nevers got the call. Tesreau, again, was ready, and Nevers was bounced back as though he had hit a stone wall. Nevers then passed into the end zone with no receiver in the area. Coach Warner said he had called a running play, but Nevers' dazed condition caused him to miss the signal.

In the fourth quarter Tesreau's brother, Louis, intercepted a pass and returned it 60 yards to give Washington a 13-0 lead. Guttormsen intercepted Nevers late in the game, and Washington had the first great victory in its short history.

The next week Washington beat California 7-0 in Berkeley before 80,000 fans and ended the season two weeks later with a 15-14 win over Oregon. With a 10-0-1 overall record and a 5-0 conference mark, Washington won the Pacific Coast Conference championship while leading the nation in scoring for a second consecutive season. The Huskies went on to face Alabama in the Rose Bowl, losing 20-19 in one of the greatest games ever played in Pasadena on New Year's Day.

Bagshaw coached Washington for four more seasons, posting an 8-2 record in 1926 and a 9-2 mark in 1927. But neither team managed to win the conference title and return to the Rose Bowl. After opening the 1927 season with five consecutive victories, the Huskies attracted another crowd of 35,000 when they shutout Washington State 14-0. In 1929, Bagshaw's last season, the Huskies averaged more than 15,000 fans for each of the five home games.

As popular as the Huskies were, their appeal could be matched by an international hero such as Colonel Charles Lindbergh. When he spoke at the stadium on September 13, 1927, more than 25,000 admirers turned out to hear the famous aviator. Following his historic flight across the Atlantic

The 1926 Rose Bowl MVP, George Wilson, was inducted into the game's Hall of Fame in 1991.

ROSE BOWL
HALL OF FAME

GEORGE WILSON
Washington

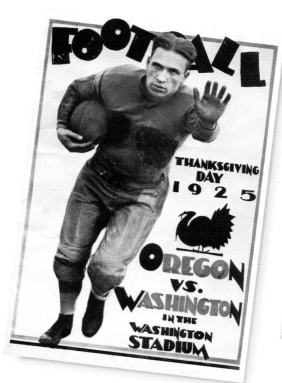

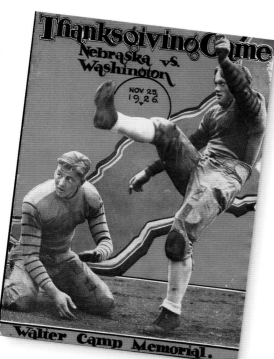

in May of that year, he piloted the Spirit of St. Louis on a nationwide tour to barnstorm for improved airfields. The huge crowd cheered as he swooped down over the stadium in his flashing silver aircraft, waving and smiling to the crowd. He then turned north to land at Sand Point Naval Station and was driven back to the stadium for his speech.

Charles Lindbergh spoke to 25,000 admirers at the stadium on September 13, 1927 after landing his plane, Spirit of St. Louis, at nearby Sand Point Naval Station.

Husky Coach Jim Phelan (below) coached from 1930 to 1941. The Huskies and Cougars played for the first time in 1934 for the Governor's Trophy (right), so named because the state's governor presents it to the victorious team following the annual showdown.

ASSOCIATED STUDENTS No. 1195

University of Washington
FOOTBALL SEASON TICKET

19 30

SEC. 22

ROW G

SEAT 23

Admit to all regularly scheduled Varsity and Freshman football games held in the University of Washington Stadium during the season of 1930.
TAX EXEMPT

Price $10.00

In 1930, Jim Phelan began a 12-year stint as Washington's head coach. In his first year, a new attendance record of 42,000 was established when the Cougars of Washington State came to Seattle to face the Huskies in the popular intrastate series. The men from the Palouse won 3-0 to claim the Governor's Trophy. It would be 11 years before Washington played a home game before a larger crowd.

The advent of the Associated Press college football rankings in 1936 set up the first game of nationally-ranked opponents in Husky Stadium. On November 14 of that year, the 10th-ranked Huskies blanked 15th-ranked Southern California 12-0. Less than two weeks later in the season finale, Husky Stadium would feature another pairing of top-ranked teams.

In the opening game of that season, Minnesota had beaten Washington, 14-7, at Husky Stadium. The Gophers would go on to win the national championship. But led by consensus All-American guard Max Starcevich, All-Coast running back Jim Cain and tackle Vic Markov, the 1936 Husky team recovered to record five shutouts and a 6-1-1 overall record. In conference play, Washington's only blemish was a 14-14 tie with Stanford.

Washington had risen to sixth in the national rankings when it faced 20th-ranked Washington State in the final regular-season game. With a Rose Bowl bid on the line, a crowd of 40,735 turned out for the Thanksgiving Day affair.

40 WASHINGTON 00:00 .... **00** WASH. STATE

NOVEMBER 26, 1936

The Perfect Game

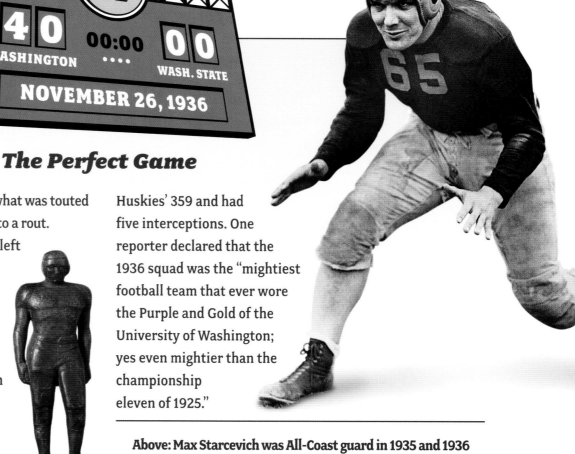

Washington State came into the game trailing the first-place Huskies by one game in the conference standings. It was the first time the cross-state rivals would battle for the conference championship. But what was touted as the national game-of-the-day turned into a rout.

Husky fullback Al Cruver blasted over left guard for the game's first touchdown. Less than three minutes later, he broke through a huge hole for a 15-yard scoring run. The Huskies built its first half lead to 20-0 when Husky quarterback Fritz Waskowitz found a wide open Byron Haines for a 37-yard touchdown pass.

The Huskies scored twice more in the fourth quarter before Cruver finished his remarkable performance for the day by scoring a third touchdown. He intercepted a Cougar throw at the 34-yard line and rumbled into the end zone for the final Husky touchdown.

The victory can be considered the most dominant in the series to that point. The Cougars did not register a first down until the final quarter and recorded only two first downs in the game. They never got into Washington territory; the closest they came was their own 44-yard line. Washington State gained only 61 total yards to the Huskies' 359 and had five interceptions. One reporter declared that the 1936 squad was the "mightiest football team that ever wore the Purple and Gold of the University of Washington; yes even mightier than the championship eleven of 1925."

Above: Max Starcevich was All-Coast guard in 1935 and 1936 and consensus All-American in 1936. He played in the 1937 Rose Bowl and in the fourth Chicago All-Star game (1937) that pitted the defending NFL champions against recently graduated college stars. The 1937 College All-Star team was the first to defeat the professionals, shutting out the Green Bay Packers 6-0. **Left:** The Pacific Coast Conference Trophy presented to Washington in 1936. **Below:** A record crowd of almost 37,000 jammed Husky Stadium for the 1936 season opener with Minnesota. The Gophers won 14-0, the Huskies' only regular season loss on their way to the Pacific Coast Conference title and a trip to the 1937 Rose Bowl.

HUSKY STADIU

The mighty Huskies, though, fell short in the 1937 Rose Bowl. Allowed to select their opponent, they passed on LSU, the popular choice, and selected Pittsburgh instead. Coach Jock Sutherland's Panthers proved to be too much, and the Huskies fell 21-0.

The growing popularity of Husky football led to the first major expansion of the stadium. In 1937, 14 rows of seats in 20 sections were added above the original bowl. The additional 10,000 seats increased capacity to 40,000. The work also resulted in a new ticket office, concession stands, broadcast and public-address systems, and spotlights. A game with Minnesota drew a record crowd of 43,000 to Husky Stadium for the 1941 season opener. A month later, 42,000 packed the stadium for a match-up with Stanford.

After the 1936 season, Coach Phelan finished his last five seasons with a 26-18-3 record. The

Left: Washington tackle Vic Markov played in the 1937 Rose Bowl and 1938 Pineapple Bowl. He was an All-America in 1937. Markov was selected captain of the 1938 College All-Star team that defeated the Washington Redskins at Soldier's Field in Chicago, Markov's hometown. Rudy Mucha (inset) was a consensus All-American center in 1940. He helped the Huskies post five shutouts during the season. Below: Ray Frankowski was a consensus All-American guard in 1940 and 1941 and was touted as the best guard in the nation during his career. He was also a member of the Husky fencing team and was Northern Division heavyweight wrestling champion.

Huskies placed second in the conference in 1940 and were ranked 10th in the nation. Ralph "Pest" Welch coached the Huskies from 1942 to 1947, compiling a 27-20-3 record.

Not only Husky fans were turning out for football at the stadium. In the early 1930s, spurred by efforts of the *Seattle Post-Intelligencer's* Royal Brougham, a series of football games was started to benefit the P-I's

Christmas Fund for needy children. In 1931 a crowd of 15,000 attended the Thanksgiving Day game between Gonzaga University and West Seattle, won by the West Seattle Yellowjackets 13-12. One of the game's attractions was the presence of the legendary Jim Thorpe and other great players of his era. During halftime, they demonstrated the football formations of the early 1900s while wearing the uniforms of that period.

On December 10, 1932, Washington hosted West Seattle for the "city championship." The day before the game, freezing temperatures turned the stadium field into an ice rink.

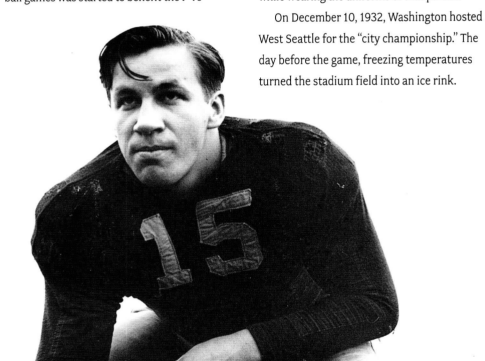

Washington coach Phelan bought tennis shoes for his players to give them better traction than cleats. Cleverly, Phelan had his troops warm up in cleats and switch to tennis shoes just before kickoff. The surer-footed Huskies rolled up a 66-0 halftime lead as Yellowjackets players slid around the field. At intermission, the West Seattle squad rounded up tennis flats, and both teams played a scoreless, shortened second half.

From 1933 to 1942, the Seattle Parent-Teachers Association joined the P-I to sponsor the charity games in the stadium. Typically held on Thanksgiving Day, the event pitted Seattle's best high school teams for the city championship.

Attendance for Husky Stadium games waned during World War II. Washington's largest home crowd was 18,561 for the annual clash with California in 1944. Husky Stadium did its patriotic duty during the war, however, by hosting a number of military-related events. In 1942 and 1943, Governor's Day saw Washington Governor Arthur Langlie, a former Husky tennis and baseball player, review assembled student military units.

Several war shows were held by military and civilian defense forces. The last was on Independence Day in 1944. The highlight was a fly-over of a Boeing B-29 Superfortress flanked by two B-17 Boeing Fortresses.

The war had an interesting impact on the Husky roster and schedule. Players who were transferred to Washington because of its campus military training program joined the team, while others left the team when called into service. Eight Washington State players suited up for the Huskies at some point during the war years when the Cougar program was suspended.

In 1943 Washington played only four regular-season games, three against military teams that often included older, more experienced college players. The best of these teams was the Fourth Air Force Flyers of March Field, CA. With a roster of collegiate standouts, the Flyers were heavily favored when they faced Washington on October 23, 1943. Husky Coach Welch devised a special defense to thwart the Flyers spread offense. Washington's Sammy Robinson scored twice and Al Akins, a Washington State transfer, returned a punt 68 yards for a score to lead the Huskies to a 27-7 upset.

Wartime travel restrictions turned the 1944 Rose Bowl into a match-up between the PCC Northern and Southern Division champions. Not having played a game since October 30, the Huskies faced a USC team that had been soundly defeated by March Field. But Washington's roster no longer included two of its key backs, Pete Susick and Jay Stoves, who were pressed into military service. The Trojans won easily, 29-0.

Designed not only for football games but for track and field events, Washington Field hosted national and international meets that featured some of the world's greatest athletes in the sport. When legendary Washington coach Hec Edmundson took over the track program in 1919, he hoped to create a West Coast relay event that would rival the popular Penn Relays in the East. The Pacific Coast Relays, later renamed the Washington Relay Carnival, was first held in the stadium in 1921. Gus Pope, a guard on the Husky football team who had won the bronze medal in the discus at the 1920 Antwerp Olympics Games, took first place in the event in the 1921 Relays. It was the first year that individual events were added to the relays format.

The popularity of The Relays attracted other track events to the stadium. In 1923, the state high school championships were held at Washington for the first time. To continue to promote the Relay Carnival, Edmundson invited

Herman Brix established a school record in the shot put at the 1928 Washington Relays and won an Olympic silver medal later that year. He twice established world records in the shot put. An outstanding tackle for Washington in 1925-1927, he played in the 1926 Rose Bowl and later earned fame as a Hollywood actor.

track and field stars from outside the Northwest. In 1924 USC sprint champ Charlie Paddock, gold medalist in the 100-meter dash and 400-meter relay at the 1920 Olympics, defeated Washington's Victor Hurley in the feature race. Two years later, Norwegian Charles Hoff, the world record holder in the pole vault, narrowly missed on his attempt to be the first man to clear 14 feet in the event.

The 1928 meet saw two of UW's great track and field heroes, Steve Anderson and Herman Brix, thrill the crowd with record-breaking performances in the 120-yard high hurdles and the shot put respectively. Both subsequently set several world records and won silver medals in the 1928 Amsterdam Olympics. The Relay Carnival

was discontinued in 1931 when all visiting teams requested that their expenses be guaranteed. That year the first annual Washington high school relay carnival was held.

The war ended the same time that Harvey Cassill became Husky athletic director. In 1948 he replaced Coach Welch with Howard Odell in a move that drew mixed reactions from Husky supporters. During Odell's five years, the Pacific Coast Conference was dominated by the California schools. Cal won in 1948, 1949, and 1950, compiling a 29-3-1 record. Stanford won in 1951 and USC in 1952. During those five years, Washington was 23-25-2.

Cassill had ambitious plans for the football program. He envisioned the Seattle community and the campus population growing and Husky Stadium expanding to meet the demand. He also realized that to draw prominent opponents, he needed more seats to enlarge gate receipts to cover the guaranteed payout. Since Washington was not drawing capacity crowds, however, critics of Cassill's expansion plan considered it a waste of resources.

As Cassill pursued his plans for the stadium, the arrival of running back Hugh McElhenny and quarterback Don Heinrich fanned new hope in Husky fans for a conference title. While McElhenny and Heinrich

Howard Odell (above left) was Washington's head football coach from 1948 to 1952. His 1950 team, featuring Don Heinrich and Hugh McElhenny, finished second in the Pacific Coast Conference. Above: Fans arrive for Washington's game against Notre Dame in 1949. The Irish won 27-7 on their way to another national championship. Don Heinrich (right) was one of the greatest quarterbacks in collegiate history. He was an All-American in 1950 and 1952. He set an NCAA record for completed passes in 1950 and led the nation in completed passes in both 1950 and 1952 and in total passing yards in 1950. Hugh McElhenny (left) was one of the finest running backs in collegiate history. He was an All-American in 1951 and set many offensive records during his career from 1949 to 1951. He still holds Husky records for most points scored by a non-kicker, longest punt return for a touchdown (100 yards) and single-game rushing yardage (296).

would finish their careers as two of the most productive offensive players in Washington's history, injuries kept them from playing together in two of their three seasons at Washington. McElhenny missed most of 1949, and a shoulder injury sidelined Heinrich in 1951. The only full year they appeared together in the backfield, in 1950, the team finished 8-2, losing only to California and Illinois, two teams that eventually met in the Rose Bowl.

Despite some criticism of Cassill's plan, the 1950 season opened with the addition of a towering upper deck to the stadium, adding 15,000 seats to its capacity. To combat the Northwest's rainy climate, a cantilevered steel roof partially covered all seats in the upper deck and approximately 6,000 in the lower sections. A two-level press box and camera deck was part of the project. Seating for about 75 members of the press provided a view 165 feet above the stadium floor. To the rear of the structure, two silo-shaped ramps provided access to the upper-deck concourses. The project, dubbed "Cassill's Castle," cost $1.7 million and was financed by ASUW funds.

Kansas State headlined the "Castle's" opening, but only 30,245 fans attended the game. No one, presumably, wanted to test the new, upper-stand seats. Those who stayed away missed a show. McElhenny set a school record by gaining 177 rushing yards on 16 carries, including a 91-yard scoring run. Heinrich threw four touchdown passes for another Husky record, including a 65-yarder to Roland Kirkby.

As part of festivities surrounding the stadium expansion, the athletic department sponsored a contest to name Washington's all-time team. Over 100,000 ballots were received and 11 players were selected and presented at halftime of the Kansas State game. The group included ends Bill Smith and Dave Nisbet, tackles Vic Markov and Paul Schwegler, guards Bill Wright and Steve Slivinski, center Walt Harrison, quarterback Wee Coyle, halfbacks George Wilson and Chuck Carroll and fullback Elmer Tesreau.

Thanks to Heinrich and McElhenny's dazzling performances, the Huskies drew a record crowd of 49,704 the next week when Minnesota came to town. The Huskies beat the 18th-ranked Gophers 28-13, recording their first win in the series in eight tries. The next week saw another Husky classic.

Harvey Cassill (right) was Washington's athletic director from 1945 to 1956. In 1950, the south upper deck was constructed (top), adding 15,000 seats and increasing stadium capacity to 55,000. The new stands earned the stadium the nickname, "Cassill's Castle." Above: With completion of the south upper deck, the field was moved 15 feet to the east to remain centered with the stadium.

GREAT GAMES

21 00:00 **20**
WASHINGTON · · · · UCLA

OCTOBER 7, 1950

Battle with the Bruins

anked 10th in the nation, Washington played its first conference game of the 1950 campaign against 13th-ranked UCLA. The small difference in poll positions would be confirmed by the end of the day.

The Bruins, coached by Red Sanders, had a high scoring, single-wing offense and one of the toughest defenses on the West Coast. UCLA took advantage of a first quarter fumble by the Huskies to jump to a 7-0 lead. The Huskies tied the score in the second period when Heinrich capped an 82-yard drive with a two-yard sneak. Washington wasted little time moving in front in the second half. On the fourth play of the quarter, Heinrich connected with Fritz Apking for a 50-yard scoring play.

Undaunted, UCLA responded on its next drive when quarterback Joe Marvin found Issac Jones in the end zone for a 38-yard score. Bob Watson missed the extra point attempt, and Washington clung to a 14-13 lead. A miscue on special teams gave

UCLA a big break in the fourth quarter. Sanders called for a short kick just over the heads of the Washington return men to pin the Huskies deep in their own territory. Instead, Anse McCullough attempted to return the boot and fumbled the ball on the Husky three-yard line. UCLA scored, giving the Bruins the lead back at 20-14.

The Husky crowd grew restless as time ticked away. Finally, Washington started a drive at its own 15-yard line with less than two minutes to play. The Huskies ground out 16 plays, including McElhenny's one-yard touchdown plunge, to even the contest. Jim Rosenzweig booted the extra point, and Washington completed a dramatic 21-20 win.

Observers of the game will never forget Washington's dramatic, second-quarter goal-line stand. With a first down on the Husky nine-yard line, the Bruins completed a pass to the Husky one but were unable to score in three attempts. Jim Wiley keyed the Husky stand by assisting with tackles on each of the goal-line stops.

Left: A 1950s-era helmet. Above: Hugh McElhenny picks up big yardage during Washington's thrilling 21-20 defeat of Pacific Coast rival UCLA Bruins in 1950.

With the addition of the upper deck in 1950, athletic department officials realized the closed end of the stadium would be the least attractive for ticket buyers. The renovation included moving the field 15 yards to the east, situating section 24 at the 50-yard line. Thus, the "Horseshoe Club" was started. Club members were treated to favors. At the Kansas State game, the first 100 women entering the section received a mum corsage. Each week a drawing was held, with the winner presented the ball from a Washington touchdown in the previous week's game. Ironically, when the stadium's north side was added in 1987, the idea was resurrected, but this time as the "Fun Zone."

Another Husky tradition, the annual Band Day, traces its origin to the Kansas State game. Conceived as a means to promote tickets sales in communities across the state, the event was originally called Western Washington Band Day. In 1952 the name changed to High School Band Day, as invitations were extended to schools in central as well as western Washington.

Even with additional supporters in the stands, Washington saw its hopes for its first Rose Bowl appearance since 1944 disappear later in the 1950 season when California defeated the Huskies 14-7 in Husky Stadium. Washington finished the year 8-2 and ranked 11th in the nation.

The 1951 season proved a disappointment as the team's record slipped to 3-6-1, but against USC, McElhenny provided one of the most thrilling individual moments ever witnessed in the stadium. Fielding a punt at his goal line instead of letting it bounce into the endzone, he broke several Trojan tackles in racing the length of the field for a touchdown.

John Cherberg, Washington's freshman coach from 1948 to 1952, became head coach in 1953. He ended a three-year stint with a 10-18-2 record, a team mutiny, his own firing, and athletic director Harvey Cassill's resignation. In the

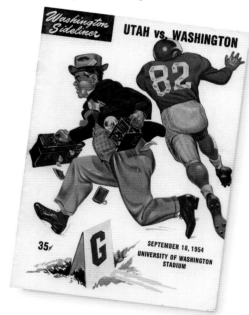

spring of 1956, Washington was placed on a three-year probation for paying players more than was allowed under conference rules. Darrell Royal coached the Huskies to a 5-5 record in 1956 before moving to the University of Texas.

To entice fans from different regions of the state to attend games in Seattle, Band Day organizers invited high school bands from far and wide to perform at Washington's home games.

In 1957, Washington hired 29-year old Jim Owens, who had been an assistant under Bear Bryant at Kentucky and Texas A&M. The bright, personable, charismatic young coach brought a boot-camp philosophy that would dramatically change Husky football. He introduced conditioning drills — sometimes called the Death March — that instilled discipline and mental and physical toughness in his team. His challenge system produced a ferocity among Husky players that would be recognized throughout the country.

In Owens' first season, Washington went 3-6-1. The following year, 1958, the Huskies had 28 sophomores on a 50-player roster. The season ended 3-7 but included wins over

Minnesota and Oregon and a close loss to the 1958 Rose Bowl champion, highly-ranked Ohio State, in Columbus.

During Owens' first season, students from the University of Alaska presented Washington with its newest mascot, an Alaskan Malamute named Denali. Dr. Harry Cross, who was a law professor on campus, assumed responsibility for acting as the dog's handler. Denali, which meant "great white one," didn't exactly meet the students' expectation as he looked more like a Fox Terrier than a Husky.

Two years later the students chose a more

Jim Owens (left) became Washington's head coach in 1957 at the age of 29. He was 99-82-6 in 18 seasons at the helm. His teams won three conference titles and played in three Rose Bowls. His 1959 team defeated Wisconsin 44-8 in the 1960 Rose Bowl, earning Washington its first Rose Bowl victory. After a victory over Minnesota in the 1961 Rose Bowl, Washington was ranked number one in the nation by the Helms Foundation. Above: Coach Owens is carried off the field after the Huskies beat the Cougars 20-0 to win the 1959 conference title and a trip to the 1960 Rose Bowl. Right: Regent Denali was the Husky mascot for 12 years starting in 1969.

suitable representative. A kennel in Olympia provided a new dog, and the football team provided the name: King Chinook. In 1969 Regent Denali started a 12-year tenure as the school's mascot.

Huskies' first conference title since 1936. Washington finished the regular season 9-1. The loss was to seventh-ranked USC in a classic match-up on October 17 in Husky Stadium.

be hard to find a club anywhere, anytime, that played a 60-minute period any better than that team that day."

Ranked third at the beginning of the 1960

"It would be hard to find a club anywhere, anytime, that played a 60-minute period any better than that team that day."

—Coach Jim Owens after Washington's 44-8 victory over Wisconsin in the 1960 Rose Bowl.

The dog received his name from the student body. They figured if the University president could have his regents, students could have one, too.

King Redoubt and Prince Redoubt followed as Dr. Cross handed over mascot duties to his son, Kim, and his family. In 1999 the latest Alaskan Malamute, Spirit, began his reign as king of the Husky sidelines. When the athletic department added a costumed mascot to provide entertainment at games, it was named Harry the Husky. The name was an indirect salute to Harry Cross' dedication to the mascot program.

In 1959, the Huskies won the conference title of the newly formed Athletic Association of Western Universities, which included the four California schools of the Pacific Coast Conference and Washington. It was the

Washington was ranked eighth after the regular season and routed Wisconsin 44-8 in the 1960 Rose Bowl. Jim Owens recalled: "It would

season, the Huskies won the first two games and then suffered a bitter 15-14 defeat to Navy on a late field goal. After a victory over Stanford in Palo Alto, Washington beat UCLA by a score of 10-8 and Oregon State, 30-29. In the UCLA game, Husky All-American quarterback Bob Schloredt broke his collarbone while playing defense. Against Oregon State, Washington won by twice completing two-point conversions. Both games were tense, as the death of two men from heart attacks during the UCLA game would attest.

Above: Husky quarterback Bob Schloredt on a rollout in Washington's smashing victory over Wisconsin in the 1960 Rose Bowl. He shared the MVP award with George Fleming in the 1960 Rose Bowl and was MVP in the 1961 Rose Bowl. Right: Bob Schloredt, on the front of the October 3, 1960 issue of *Sports Illustrated*, was the first Husky to make the magazine's cover. *SI* devoted a three-page feature to the Husky quarterback.

"*I won't say* **Owens gets the** hungriest *football players* in the West each year,

but if they were in the **Roman Coliseum,** the lions wouldn't come out."

— Jim Murray, columnist for the *Los Angeles Times,* 1963

HUSKY S T A D I U M 49

GREAT GAMES

07 00:00 **06**
WASHINGTON ···· OREGON

OCTOBER 29, 1960

Don McKeta's Determination

As long as Husky Stadium stands, Husky fans will talk about the day Don McKeta beat Oregon with one of the greatest plays in Washington history.

The setting found the ninth-ranked, 6-1 Huskies hosting the 5-1 Ducks. Despite not scoring, Washington dominated the first half of play. The Huskies gained 10 first downs while Oregon managed one. The Ducks never advanced beyond their own 38-yard line.

The Huskies missed a chance to score late in the first half. On the Oregon 25, George Fleming dropped back for a field-goal attempt. But Washington was penalized 15 yards because the kicking tee had been tossed in from the bench without being properly requested. Fleming's kick from the longer distance was no good.

Oregon took the lead when Bruce Snyder, who would later coach at California and Arizona State in the Pac-10, scored on a five-yard pitch. The Ducks failed to make the extra-point attempt but received another chance when the Huskies were penalized for being offsides. The second kick was swatted down by Ray Mansfield, who climbed the backs of interior linemen to block it.

In the fourth quarter, Bob Hivner intercepted an Oregon pass to kill a Duck drive within five yards of the Husky goal

line. Playing quarterback, he then directed Washington on a memorable drive. At midfield and facing a fourth-and-six situation with less than three minutes to play, the Huskies elected to go for it. Hivner threw a short pass to McKeta. Slanting toward the north sideline, McKeta appeared to be heading out of bounds to stop the clock.

At least, that is what Oregon defender Dave Grayson and most everyone watching thought. But McKeta had no intention of going out of bounds on his own.

His resolve was born of the UCLA game when he felt he did not give enough effort after being tackled on a critical play. So when he caught Hivner's pass, he thought only of driving upfield for the score or being knocked out of bounds. "I was lucky," McKeta said. "I was ready to step out of bounds if he (Grayson) had come after me. I saw I had a step on him so I turned the corner and ran...I thought sure I would be caught from behind." He wasn't.

Fleming, known as "Mr. Automatic," kicked the extra point, and the Huskies enjoyed a 7-6 lead. Hivner killed the Ducks' final threat when he made his third interception of the game.

Above: Don McKeta turns up field in the 1960 Oregon game. George Fleming (right) was a multi-talented member of the 1960 and 1961 Rose Bowl teams. He was the co-MVP in the 1960 Rose Bowl.

Above: 1961 cheerleaders with Husky mascot King Chinook. Cheerleaders from the era performed routines to "Bow Down to Washington" and "Victory for Washington." Later, "Tequila," "Louie Louie" and "Celebration" became signature Washington game songs. The Apple Cup Trophy (below) is awarded to the winner of the annual game between Washington and Washington State. Bill Douglas (right) was a Husky quarterback from 1962 to 1964, leading Washington to a conference title in 1963 and a trip to the Rose Bowl in 1964. He was a National Football Foundation Scholar-Athlete in 1964.

Thanks in part to McKeta's dramatic play, the Huskies returned to the Rose Bowl to face top-ranked Minnesota. After beating the Gophers 17-7, Washington was voted the national champions by the Helms Foundation, the only poll in those days that conducted its final team rankings after all bowl games were played.

Owens' teams at the start of the decade drew tremendous respect for their toughness and superior conditioning. In 1963, legendary *Los Angeles Times* columnist Jim Murray wrote, "I won't say Owens gets the hungriest football players in the West each year, but if they were in the Roman Coliseum, the lions wouldn't come out."

The 1962 season also saw an emblematic change in the Huskies' rivalry with the cross-state Cougars, as the Governor's Trophy, traditionally awarded to the winning team, was replaced by the Apple Cup. Washington took home the trophy after beating the home-standing Cougars, 26-21.

In the last 14 years of Owens' coaching tenure, the Huskies would win the conference title one more time, in 1963, and appear in one more Rose Bowl, losing to Illinois 17-7 in 1964. In 1970, Washington finished second in what was then the Pacific-8 conference.

The football team's success, including back-to-back Rose Bowl appearances, sparked interest in an upper deck for the north side of the stadium. In December 1962, Owens submitted a

HUSKY **STADIUM** 51

Stadium Addition Feasibility Survey to the Athletic Advisory Committee. In September 1965, the Board of Regents approved the plan to add 20,718 seats to the north and west sides, increasing stadium capacity to 76, 218. When construction bids were unsealed, however, the lowest was nearly $2 million more than the original estimate of $3.6 million. The expansion was considered too costly to pursue, and the plan lay dormant for 20 years.

Milestone events and individual achievements did not wait for the stadium's growth. From the advent of the Associated Press rating system in 1936, no top-ranked team ever played in Husky Stadium until 1967. That year, top-ranked USC toppled Washington 23-6. Two years later, number-one Ohio State visited Husky Stadium and defeated the Purple and Gold 41-14.

Defensive back Al Worley's game against Idaho in 1968 helped him set an NCAA record that may never be broken. Worley intercepted four passes in the game, a Husky record, during a season that saw him set an NCAA mark of 14 interceptions in 10 games.

WAKE UP, COACH. LOOK!

I FEEL A LITTLE FAINT MYSELF

TIPPS

Rick Redman (above right) was a two-time consensus All-American (1963, 1964). The Husky linebacker and punter led the 1963 team to a conference title and the 1964 Rose Bowl. He is a member of the College Football Hall of Fame. Top: Rick Redman's jersey. Above left: Bob McCausland's "Hairbreadth Husky" cartoons in the *Seattle Post-Intelligencer* often poked fun at the hometown Huskies. This cartoon appeared on December 2, 1963. Going into the final week of play, Washington had a 3-1 conference record — the loss was to UCLA — and USC was 2-1. All games were postponed for a week after President John Kennedy was assassinated in Dallas. On November 30, the Huskies beat WSU 16-0 and USC stopped UCLA 25-6. Washington was selected to go to the Rose Bowl.

east end zone. In 1969, low-level lights were mounted to the upper deck, primarily for evening soccer matches.

Coming off a 1-9 season in 1969, Husky fans held little hope for the new season with an inexperienced sophomore quarterback at the helm. What they got was a legend. Sonny Sixkiller's debut was one of the most stunning in the annals of the program. Directing a wide-open passing attack, Sixkiller led Washington to a

In fall 1968, a radical change occurred on the stadium field. Washington became the first college in the country to install AstroTurf, a new synthetic playing surface. Because of the lack of similar surfaces in other stadiums, the Husky equipment room stocked over 200 pairs of shoes for opponents to use during games. The original artificial turf was replaced in 1972, 1977, 1987 and 1995.

Stadium capacity increased from 55,000 to more than 59,000 in 1968 when 4,000 seats were added to the north side and portable bleachers were installed beyond the

lopsided 42-16 victory over Michigan State in the 1970 opener.

He would set a number of passing records and finish his Washington career with more yards throwing (5,496) than any previous Husky player. His exploits and popularity inspired a Sonny Sixkiller T-shirt, fan club and a song recorded by a local disc jockey. Sixkiller's play in Washington's classic slugfest with Purdue helped him become just the second Husky player to grace the cover of *Sports Illustrated*.

Top: Husky cheerleaders dance in the rain during the 1964 Oregon game. Above: Tom Greenlee was a consensus All-American defensive end in 1966. He began his career as a running back on the freshmen squad and then moved to the defensive secondary. He also returned kicks. Left: Nicknamed "The Thief," Al Worley was a consensus All-American defensive back in 1968. He set an NCAA record that year of 14 interceptions and finished his Husky career with 18. That mark and his four pick-offs in one game are Husky records.

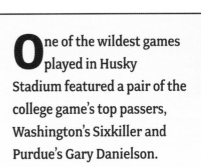

GREAT GAMES

W

38 00:00 **35**
WASHINGTON ···· PURDUE

SEPTEMBER 18, 1971

Huskies Come From Behind Four Times

One of the wildest games played in Husky Stadium featured a pair of the college game's top passers, Washington's Sixkiller and Purdue's Gary Danielson.

Washington lit up the scoreboard first when Sixkiller connected with receiver Tom Scott on a fourth-down play. Trailing 7-0 after one quarter, Danielson faked a handoff and then pitched the ball to wideout Darryl Stingley for a 17-yard scoring run. With 5:30 left in the half, Purdue picked off a Sixkiller pass, and Danielson gave the Boilermakers the lead when he scampered 43 yards for a score.

Things were just getting interesting. Four plays later Scott took a handoff on a reverse and raced 60 yards to tie the game. With nine seconds left in the half, UW's Steve Wiezbowski made a 32-yard field goal to give Washington a 17-14 halftime lead.

The seesaw battle continued early in the third quarter when Purdue's Otis Armstrong scored on a 39-yard run. Washington regained the lead 24-21 on Jerry Ingalls' dive into the end zone. Sixkiller made four long passes on third downs to keep that scoring drive alive. Late in the quarter, powered by Armstrong's running, the Boilermakers reclaimed the lead at 28-24.

Once again the Huskies responded with another touchdown run by Ingalls with 13 minutes to play. With Washington holding a 31-28 lead, each team's defense finally managed to stop the other's potent offense. With 3:39 to play, Danielson found Stingley open behind the Washington secondary, and he raced untouched for an 80-yard score to put Purdue ahead, 35-31.

Washington had one last comeback left. Heeding the advice of Coach Owens to "stay cool and score," Sixkiller needed just five plays to get the Huskies back in the end zone. This time it was a 33-yard pass to Scott for the winning score. The game was still in doubt until Husky linebacker Rick Huget picked off a Danielson pass late in the contest. Owens called it the best come-from-behind game in his 15 years of Husky coaching.

Sixkiller and his classmates would compile a 22-10 record before they graduated. Only Stanford with Heisman winner Jim Plunkett in 1970 and the "Thunderchickens" in 1971 and the 1972 USC national champions kept Washington from the Rose Bowl during the three-year period.

While Sixkiller was attracting a cult following, legends of track and field returned to the stadium oval. Cassill's plans to improve the stature of Husky athletics included bringing NCAA championships to Seattle. He succeeded by attracting the college

Above: Husky quarterback Sonny Sixkiller drops back to pass. Sixkiller's popularity spawned a record, The Ballad of Sonny Sixkiller; hot-selling "6-Killer" T shirts; and a "6-Killer" fan club. **Left:** Helmet belonging to Robin Earl, Husky tight end and fullback from 1973 to 1976 and 1976 team co-captain.

Don James, who became Husky head coach in 1975, compiled a 153-57-2 record in his 18 years at Washington, making him the winningest football coach in Husky history. His 99 Pac-10 victories were the most in conference history. He took his teams to 15 bowl games (10-5) including a Pac-10-record nine straight from 1979 to 1987. He guided the Huskies to six Rose Bowl games and is one of only four coaches to notch four Rose Bowl victories.

basketball Final Four tournament in 1949, won by the Kentucky Wildcats, and in 1952, won by the Kansas Jayhawks, and the 1951 track and field championship, won by USC. Twenty years later, its cross-town rival, UCLA, finished first when the event returned to the stadium. Sixteen stadium records were smashed in the 1971 event. Highlighting the meet was Marty Liquori running the stadium's first sub-four minute (3:57.6) mile.

The following summer saw the University host the 1972 AAU Track and Field Championships. Outstanding performances included Dave Roberts' clearing 18 feet in the pole vault; Lee Evans, the 400-meter world-record holder and 1968 Mexico City Olympic Games gold medalist, winning that competition; Rod Milburn racing to victory in the high hurdles; and Dave Wottle, wearing his signature cap, winning the 800-meter run.

After disappointing seasons in 1973 and 1974, Owens announced his retirement from coaching at the team's banquet on November 27, 1974. During his 18 years at Washington, he had brought respectability and ferocity back to West Coast football.

A month later, Don James, head coach at Kent State, was named Husky head coach. James' coaching style contrasted sharply with Owens.' James' trademark was a thorough, detailed approach to practices, game preparation and situation analysis. He hired good coaches, managed them well and had the ability to get the most from his assistants and players. As Chuck Nelson, a Husky All-American kicker, said: "You knew exactly what was expected of you and when it was expected. Everybody respected him (James) because you couldn't fault him for anything."

After his first two seasons, the Huskies' record stood at 11-11, and the team started the 1977 season at 1-3. Fans and the media were growing skeptical of James' coaching ability and his selection of Warren Moon as the Husky quarterback, and stadium attendance was dropping. Then came a huge 54-0 victory at Oregon, followed by victories at Stanford and Oregon State. After a tough loss to UCLA in Los Angeles, Washington traveled to Berkeley and beat California, earning James national coach-of-the-week honors. The Husky bandwagon started to fill up quickly as traditional nemesis USC came to town.

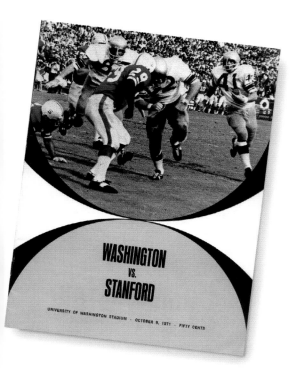

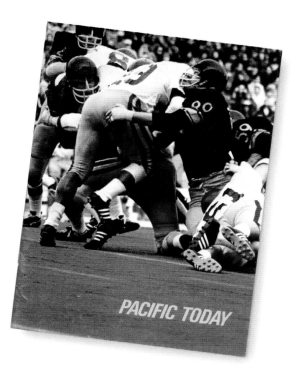

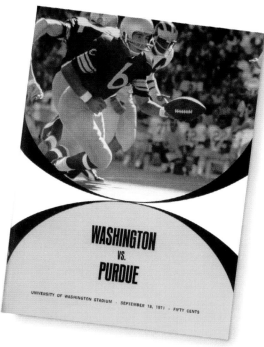

GREAT GAMES
W

28
WASHINGTON
00:00
••••
10
USC

NOVEMBER 12, 1977

Warren Moon's Long Touchdown Run Tramples Trojans

Before the largest Husky Stadium crowd in five years, Washington faced 14th-ranked USC in a game that opened the door for the first Rose Bowl appearance of a James-coached team. The Huskies and Trojans entered the game tied with UCLA for the conference lead.

USC's powerful offense featured tailback Charles White, the nation's leading rusher, and quarterback Rob Hertel. The Trojans were coming off a 49-0 blowout of Stanford, where they gained 592 yards of total offense.

Special-teams play by the Huskies and turnovers prevented USC from getting its high-powered offense in gear. The hard-hitting Huskies recovered three of six Trojan fumbles, intercepted Hertel three times and blocked two punts. Junior linebacker Michael

Jackson was the Huskies' star. He intercepted two passes, recovered one fumble and led the Huskies in tackles.

Holding a slim, 7-3 lead, Washington sprang to life in the second half as heavy rains and strong winds pelted the field. Warren Moon found Spider Gaines in the end zone for a 19-yard score. Linebacker Mike Rohrbach blocked a Trojan punt to set up Joe Steele's one-yard scoring plunge to give the Huskies a commanding 21-3 lead.

Trying to run out the clock late in the game, Moon broke free for a 71-yard touchdown to give the Huskies the 28-10 victory. It still stands as the longest run by a quarterback in Washington's history. Husky running back Joe Steele had an outstanding day, rushing for 106 yards.

The next week the Huskies beat Washington State 35-15 and then had to wait six days for the outcome of the UCLA-USC game to determine the conference title. In a classic matchup, USC's Frank Jordan kicked a 38-yard field goal with two seconds remaining that gave his team a dramatic 29-27 victory. After 14 years, Washington was back in the Rose Bowl. The Huskies made the most of the opportunity, defeating fourth-ranked Michigan 27-20.

The 1977 campaign marked the beginning of a remarkable run of winning seasons for the Husky program that extends to the current era. Washington tied for second in the conference, now expanded to the Pacific-10, in 1978 and 1979 and beat Texas in the 1979 Sun Bowl, 14-7. The Huskies won the conference championship in 1980, losing to Michigan 23-6 in the 1981 Rose Bowl.

In 1981, Washington again won the Pac-10 title. The Huskies faced third-ranked USC in its next to last game of the season. On a soggy day at Husky Stadium when gusty winds forced the closure of Evergreen Point Bridge, the Huskies

Husky quarterback Warren Moon (above) scored two touchdowns in Washington's 28-10 defeat of USC. The victory secured a trip to the 1978 Rose Bowl, the first appearance at the Pasadena classic for a Don James' team. Right: The uniform hat worn by Bill Cole, the Husky Marching Band's director from 1957 to 1969. He introduced innovative routines and Husky favorites such as "Everything's Coming up Roses" and "California Here I Come."

beat the Trojans 13-3. While the Huskies didn't stop USC running back Marcus Allen from becoming the first collegian to rush for 2,000 yards in a single season, they did prevent USC from scoring a touchdown for the first time since 1967. Washington's Fred Small scored the game's only touchdown when he recovered a misplayed kickoff in the end zone.

Growing with Washington's football fortunes was the Husky Marching Band, with a history as fascinating as the team's. During the first 14 years that the school fight song, "Bow Down to Washington," was played, an ROTC military unit performed the tune. Though there are accounts of a band playing at the historic 1902 game with Nevada, it wasn't until 1929 that the first school band was assembled under

the direction of Walter Welke. He started with a unit of 26 performers that grew to a 127-member ensemble by the time the team went to the 1937 Rose Bowl. During the band's second year, Helen Bassetti joined as its first majorette.

Welke's bands became the first on the West Coast to march through various formations while playing. The band also organized colorful halftime routines in collaboration with the student card section. The war thinned the ranks of the band, but Welke rebuilt it afterward and served as director until Bill Cole replaced him following the 1956 football season. In 1965 Cole hired an assistant director, Bill Bissell, who became band director in 1970. Halftime shows at Washington have never been the same.

Bissell believed the band should be both entertaining and fun, and halftime routines became "theatre in the round." Theme shows and outrageous costumes were com-

Above: Uniform worn by the drum major in the Husky Marching Band in the late 1950s. Above left: The Husky Band under Walter Welke organized colorful half-time routines with the student card section. For 24 years starting in 1970, Bill Bissell (below) directed the Husky Band program as one of the great showmen among collegiate band directors. He and yell leader Robb Weller started a worldwide staple of sports, the spectator-coordinated WAVE, in 1981.

monplace. "Tequila" and "Louie, Louie" became so popular they took on the status of school songs. Bissell's band started a tradition of performing "The Stripper" the last time members wore a set of uniforms. As the performance wound down, they slowly peeled off their soon-to-be retired togs.

Bissell was not afraid to poke fun at an opponent. In a game with California, the band spelled out BEERS, then BARES before finally coming together to form the correct BEARS. The director once had the band form SILO TECH during an Apple Cup performance of Washington State's fight song.

Washington was blessed to have energetic yell leader Robb Weller pumping enthusiasm into the student section in the early 1970s. Weller's command of the crowd allowed him to start a sporting tradition that became a ritual at sports events worldwide. Weller's original idea was to have the crowd stand rapidly from the lowest seats to the highest, creating a huge ripple effect in the stadium. Despite numerous attempts, he

and Bissell could not effectively coordinate the stunt.

Returning for the 1981 homecoming game with Stanford, Weller and Bissell teamed up again. Weller sprinted down the sideline to the east end of the stadium and instructed the crowd to start rising in that section and create a human wave that rolled around Husky Stadium. It worked, and The Wave was introduced to college football on October 31, 1981. It is believed to have started in the third quarter as the Huskies reeled off 28 points en route to a 42-31 win over the John Elway-led opponent.

In 2001, Weller and Bissell returned to Husky Stadium to mark the 20th anniversary of The Wave. With the Huskies leading 10th-ranked Stanford 28-20 after three quarters, Bissell and Weller recreated the scene from the 1981 con-

test, leading the crowd in a Wave that ran all the way around Husky Stadium and spurred Washington to 14 more points in the fourth quarter on the way to a 42-28 upset. But back to 1981, the Husky faithful had plenty to cheer about in the season finale.

Top: Husky fans watched Bill Bissell's bands recreate the Mt. St. Helens eruption, stage horse races, and wear outrageous costumes. Above: Former Husky male and female letter winners form two lines outside the tunnel to greet the Huskies for the second half of the Homecoming game each year.

23 WASHINGTON 00:00 •••• **10** WASH. STATE

NOVEMBER 21, 1981

Another Disappointment for the Cougars

When Washington State and Washington met in the 1981 Apple Cup, it was billed as the biggest game in the series since the 1936 game when the winner traveled to the Rose Bowl. The Cougars entered the game 8-1-1, and 5-1-1 in conference play. The Huskies were 8-2, with a 5-2 Pac-10 record. Washington State was ranked 14th in the nation; the Huskies were 17th. Washington's defense was the best in the league, while the Cougars ranked high in the offensive categories.

The outcome of the UCLA-USC game, which started 40 minutes before the Husky kickoff, also had an impact on

Above: Paul Skansi makes a diving catch in the end zone with eight seconds left in the half in Washington's 23-10 win over the Cougars in 1981 to clinch the conference title. Right: Chuck Nelson was a consensus All-American place kicker in 1982. He holds the Husky record for most points by a kicker in a season: 109 his senior year. Also, in 1982, Nelson converted 25 of 26 field goals for a .962 percentage, an NCAA record. He still holds the NCAA record for 30 consecutive field goals in 1981-82. His .819 career field-goal percentage is the best in Husky and Pac-10 history.

the game. The Huskies needed the Trojans to upset UCLA to clear the way for a Rose Bowl bid. With so much at stake, there was plenty of scoreboard watching by the frenzied Husky faithful.

His team trailing 7-3 late in the second quarter, Husky quarterback Steve Pelluer fired a low pass towards wideout Paul Skansi. Washington State cornerback Nate Bradley looked as if he would smother the ball when Skanski dove over the defender for an amazing catch in the end zone.

Washington State drove the ball 69 yards to open the second half and tie the score at 10. From that point the Huskies, behind the fine play of their offensive line, took control. Ron "Cookie" Jackson capped an 80-yard march by running 23 yards to put the Huskies ahead 17-10. Following a Cougar turnover, All-American kicker Chuck Nelson booted his second a field goal of the game to increase the Huskies' lead to 10 points.

The fate of the Cougars was sealed when the final score of the USC-UCLA game was announced. The Trojans had engineered an upset. The crowd went wild. Nelson added a field goal with less than three minutes to play, and the Huskies were off to the Rose Bowl. Jackson, with 103 yards, and Jacque Robinson, with 93, accounted for almost two-thirds of Washington's 302 total rushing yards.

At the 1982 Rose Bowl, Washington capitalized on the MVP performance of Robinson to shut out Iowa 28-0. The freshman running back gained 142 yards on 20 carries. Thanks in part to the Rose Bowl win, the Huskies entered the 1982 season ranked second in the preseason wire service standings. For the first time in school history, Washington played a game at home as the nation's top-ranked team when the

Huskies beat Oregon 37-21 on September 25.

Later in the season, Husky Stadium was the site of one of its greatest celebrations, and the team was not even playing there that day. With both schools in contention for the Pac-10 title, Washington's road game at third-ranked

Arizona State was broadcast back to campus on closed-circuit television. An overflow crowd in Edmundson Pavilion forced the setup of a second screen in the stadium. After the Huskies clinched a 17-13 victory, fans stormed the Husky Stadium goal posts and tore them from the ground.

From 1982 to 1989, James' teams would compile a 65-28-2 record and appear in seven

Left: Ron Holmes was a consensus All-American defensive lineman in 1984. He was named Most Valuable Lineman in Washington's 28-17 victory against Oklahoma in the 1985 Orange Bowl. Holmes received the Morris Trophy in 1984 as the Pac-10's top defensive lineman. Below: Quarterback Chris Chandler engineered a 99-yard drive with four minutes to play to gain a dramatic victory over USC in 1985. Bottom right: Jeff Jaeger was a consensus All-American place kicker in 1986. He is the all-time Husky scoring leader with 358 points and 80 career field goals. Bottom: Football kicked by Jeff Jaeger to set an NCAA record of 80 career field goals.

postseason bowl games. In 1984, Washington would lose only one game, 16-7, to USC in the Los Angeles Coliseum, finish second to the Trojans in the conference and beat second-ranked Oklahoma in the Orange Bowl, 28-17. The Huskies would finish second in the nation, the highest ranking in school history at the time.

That era also showcased some of the greatest comebacks in the stadium's history. In 1983 Steve Pelluer directed a near-flawless late-game drive to rally Washington to a 25-24 victory over Michigan. In a brilliant performance, he completed his final 14 passes of the game, including all eight on the last drive. With 34 seconds remaining, he tossed a seven-yard scoring strike to Mark Pattison to cap the Huskies' 80-yard drive. Don James didn't hesitate to go for the two-point conversion and victory. Pelluer found tight-end Larry Michael for the winning conversion.

Down 17-13 with four minutes to play against the Trojans in 1985, Washington appeared doomed to defeat when USC came to the line of scrimmage on the Huskies' one-yard line. Instead, USC tailback Ryan Knight, who had rushed for 135 yards, fumbled and gave

Washington hope. Quarterback Chris Chandler connected with receiver Lonzell Hill to convert a pair of fourth-down plays and march the Huskies to the 13-yard line. Chandler, a sopho-

more making his first start, connected one more time with Hill in the game's closing seconds for a dramatic 20-17 victory.

In 1988 the Huskies found themselves trailing California 27-3 when they scored 25 points

in 20 minutes to record the greatest come-from-behind win in school history. Quarterback Cary Conklin was one of the heroes, throwing for 315 yards. Kicker John McCallum booted the deciding field goal with less than a minute to play.

Some feel the best rally of the Don James era occurred in his first season as head coach in 1975. Washington trailed Washington State 27-14 with 3:01 to play and the Cougars on the Huskies' 14-yard line. At the urging of his players, WSU coach Jim Sweeney decided against a field goal on fourth-and-one and went with a pass play. Washington's Al Burleson intercepted and darted 93 yards for a score.

With time winding down, the Huskies got the ball back, and quarterback Warren Moon tossed a deep pass that bounced off a Cougar defender into the arms of Spider Gaines. He raced into the end zone to

cap a 78-yard play and give James what he would later call the most memorable win in his career.

Conklin engineered another classic comeback when he led Washington to a thrilling 28-27 victory against UCLA in 1989. After falling behind 21-0 in the first quarter, the Huskies calmly whittled away at the Bruin lead. Conklin was masterful on the winning drive late in the contest, hitting four of six passes. Greg Lewis rumbled in from the 10-yard line for the final score with a minute to play.

Conklin's passing and Lewis' running played big roles in Washington's 34-7 trouncing of Florida at the 1989 Freedom Bowl. The Husky defense provided a preview of things to come when it limited Florida All-American running back Emmett Smith to 17 yards. Something spe-

cial was about to occur near Montlake Cut.

The stadium's current symmetry arrived in 1987 when the upper deck and roof were added to the north side. From the top of the roof to the field below, the stadium was the height of a 16-story building. Its capacity grew to 72,500 with the addition of 13,000 seats at a cost of $17.7 million. At the time, Husky Stadium was the largest college facility in the nation. With 70 percent of the seats located between the end zones, it had also become one of the loudest.

Completion of the upper deck in time for a September 5 dedication game against Stanford became a huge concern when, on February 25, several sections of steel framing collapsed in a heap.

Thanks to an accelerated construction schedule, inspectors gave final approval to the north deck the morning of the game. In the event the stadium had not been ready, early-season tickets included seat locations for both Husky Stadium and the Kingdome.

Most of the financing for the north upper deck was provided by donors who purchased seating rights to the Tyee Center, an endzone-to-endzone gathering place on the second level of the new addition. Later renamed the Don James Center in honor of the retired Husky football coach, the center provided the athletic department a colorful venue for gatherings, banquets, press conferences, team meals, department meetings and, occasionally, weddings for true Husky fans.

The most recent major construction in Husky Stadium was the replacement of the west stands in 1989. The $3.7 million project gave Husky fans better seating and more concession

Above: Reggie Rogers, a basketball standout, was a consensus All-American defensive lineman in 1986. That year he was named the Morris Trophy winner as top defensive lineman in the Pac-10. Left: Several sections of steel framing collapsed in a heap during construction of the north-side upper deck in 1987.

stands and restrooms and provided a photo deck on top of the west scoreboard. During the summer of 1990, new aluminum seating replaced the wooden bleachers in the north upper deck. The same process took place on the south upper deck in the summer of 1992.

The look of the playing field greatly improved in 2000 when a revolutionary new playing surface, FieldTurf, replaced the harder, less-forgiving artificial turf. Openly welcomed by Husky players, FieldTurf gave the appearance of real grass while using a sand-and-rubber-pellet base for solid traction and a softer surface. Washington followed Nebraska as the second major college to play on the surface.

To ease congestion for the growing number of fans attending games in the expanded stadium, the athletic department worked with the city's bus system to improve its "park-and-ride" program. Fans could go to designated Metro bus lots for a free ride to the game. More than

15,000 customarily take advantage of the service.

Boat traffic for games also grew considerably, with nearly 300 moorage passes being issued annually. The maritime tradition that started when the stadium first opened grew more popular as the tour-boat industry in the region developed. By the 1950s, fans were arriving in a variety of colorful craft. With the stadium expansion in 1987, it was estimated that on a nice-weather day up to 5,000 spectators arrive by boat. It was a picture-perfect day for boating, and for being a Husky fan, when USC came to Seattle for an early-season Pac-10 showdown in 1990.

Attending the games via boat has been a tradition for decades. Below, the faithful are shown sterngating through Montlake Cut in the 1950s.

31 00:00 **00**
WASHINGTON ···· USC

SEPTEMBER 22, 1990

"All I Saw Was Purple"

Heading into the 1990 season, the winner of the USC-Washington game had gone to the Rose Bowl 10 of the previous 13 seasons. While the 1990 match was an early-season affair, it would prove to substantiate that trend.

Washington selected the game to celebrate its 100th season of football. The All-Centennial team was feted the night before and introduced at halftime of the game. Two members of the historic team, Hugh McElhenny and Nesby Glasgow, delivered inspirational talks to the team the day before the game. The Huskies, in turn, presented a gift to adoring fans. On a bright sunny day with the temperature reaching 92 degrees, the crowd of 72,617 eagerly awaited the contest.

They could not have imagined the outcome. For just the third time in 23 seasons, the Huskies shutout USC, handing the Trojans their worst conference defeat in 30 years. "Student Body Right" was held to only 28 rushing yards as the Husky defense dominated the line of scrimmage. "I've never

been shutout in my entire life," said USC quarterback Todd Marinovich. "It's never over until it's over, but this game was over really early."

Greg Lewis, the Doak Walker Award winner as the nation's top running back, gained 126 rushing yards, and sophomore quarterback Mark Brunell threw for 197 yards as the Huskies rolled to a 24-0 halftime lead. The Husky defense, led by All-American lineman Steve Emtman, stopped everything the Trojans attempted. During the first two quarters, USC had two first downs and 43 yards of total offense. Of its 22 first-half plays, 13 produced no gain or a loss of yardage.

The defense would hold USC to 163 total yards and seven first downs for the game. They would record three sacks and put so much pressure on Marinovich that after the game, weary and beaten, he said: "I just saw purple. That's all. No numbers, just purple." Washington finished the season 9-2 and beat Iowa 46-34 in the New Year's Day Classic.

The most-watched event ever held at Husky Stadium took place in the summer of 1990 when the Goodwill Games was staged in Seattle. Spanning 17 days, the competition involved 2,500 athletes from 33 countries participating in 21 sports. Opening and closing ceremonies and the track-and-field events were held in Husky Stadium. More than 70,000 spectators attended the opening ceremonies on July 21 when former President Ronald Reagan officially welcomed the Games.

The five days of track-and-field competition at the Stadium featured many world-record holders and past and future Olympic champions. Spectators were thrilled to see Jackie Joyner-Kersee, Patti Sue Plummer, Michael Johnson, Roger Kingdom, Carl Lewis and world-class athletes from other countries. The only world record in track-and-

continued on page 66

Above: Greg Lewis ran for 126 yards on 26 carries, including a long romp in the third quarter, in the Huskies' dominating defeat of USC in 1990. Lewis received the Doak Walker Award as the nation's top running back in 1990. **Right:** More than 70,000 jammed Husky Stadium on July 21, 1990 for opening ceremonies of the Goodwill Games.

HUSKY S T A D I U M

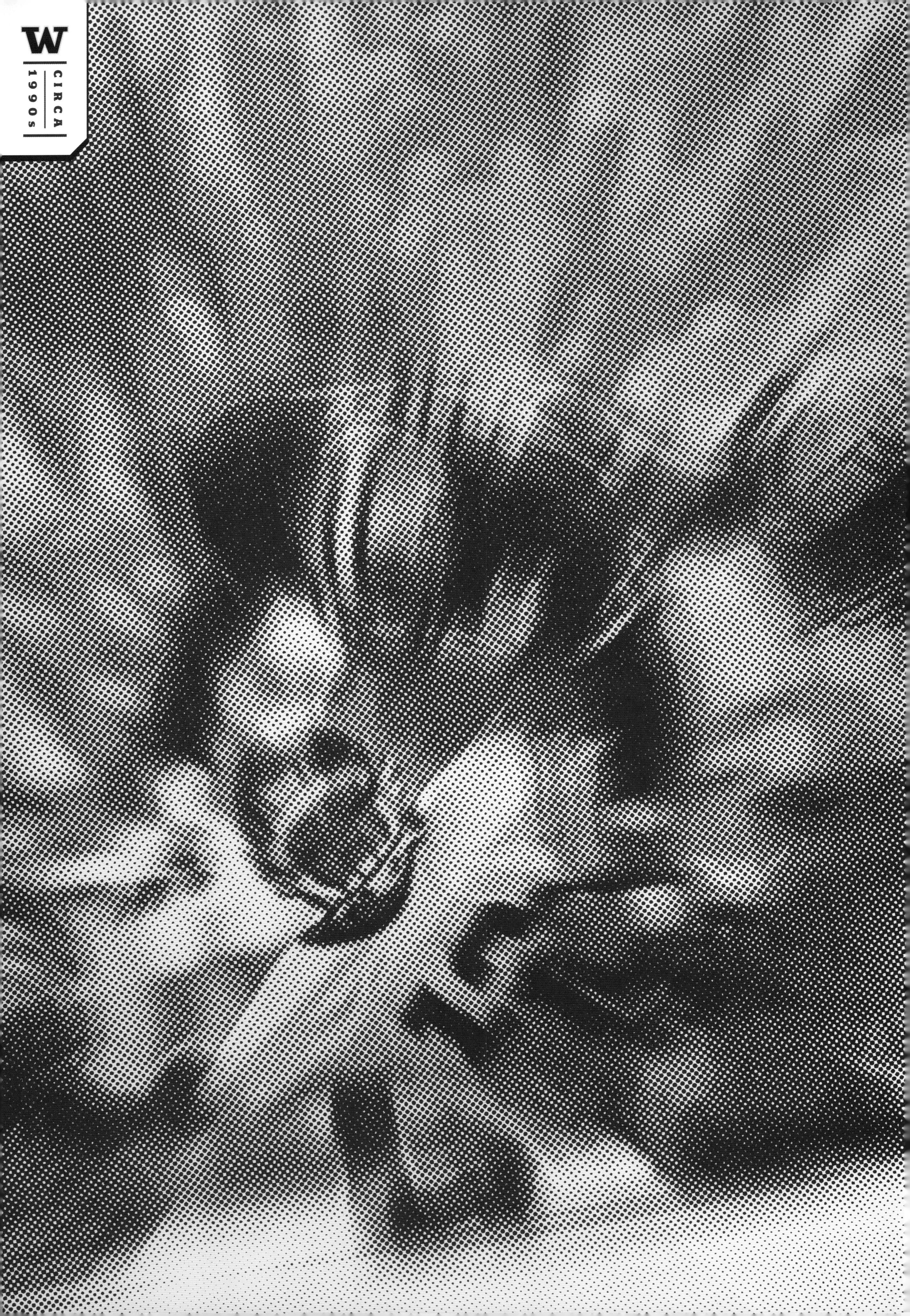

"I just saw purple. That's all. No numbers, just purple."

— USC quarterback Todd Marinovich after their 31-0 defeat by the Huskies in 1990

HUSKY STADIUM

field set at the Goodwill Games was by the Soviet Union's Nadezhda Ryashkina in the 10,000 meter race walk: a time of 41 minutes, 56.21 seconds. She broke Australian Kerry Saxby's record of 42:25.2.

Husky Stadium has also been the site for races that featured far-from-world-class athletes. Numerous benefit road races have used the stadium as a staging area and finish line, allowing local runners to compete, albeit briefly, in the stadium. The biggest such race is the annual "Nordstrom Beat the Bridge" run that has raised millions of dollars for diabetes research.

Professional athletes have been a less-common sight in the stadium. That almost changed in the 1950s when community leaders began to lobby for a professional football franchise in Seattle, and Husky Stadium was used for several National Football League (NFL) exhibition games.

Under the sponsorship of Greater Seattle, Inc., the first game was played on August 20, 1955 between the New York Giants and San Francisco Forty-Niners. A crowd of 49,000 watched former Husky quarterback Don Heinrich lead the Giants to a 28-17 victory. His former Husky teammate, 49er running back Hugh McElhenny, did not play because of an injury. On the sidelines in street clothes, McElhenny received a thunderous ovation from the crowd in the pre-game introductions.

On August 17, 1963, the American Football League's Kansas City Chiefs beat the Oakland Raiders 35-21 in an exhibition game that saw a portion of the game's proceeds aid Brian Sternberg, the Husky world-record-holding pole vaulter. He had been permanently paralyzed on July 2 of that year in a trampoline accident. That spring, the sophomore had broken the world record three times and won the NCAA and AAU championships.

At halftime, a group of track-and-field greats participated in an exhibition. John Pennell, who had broken Sternberg's mark of 16 feet, 8 inches a few weeks earlier, vaulted 16-6 to establish a new stadium record. He made his last jumps while marching bands paraded nearby and the second half of the game had begun. In the running of the "Brian Sternberg Mile,"

former Oregon great Jim Grelle set a stadium record with a time of 4:04.4.

In the mid 1960's, many in the Seattle area, including several legislators, pushed for the University to lease Husky Stadium in order to attract a professional football franchise. In December 1965, the University's Board of Regents took a firm stand against the use of the stadium for professional events. Such use, they stated, would neither be to the financial advantage of the University nor consistent with its purposes and values.

Shortly afterward, plans were developed for a publicly financed multi-purpose stadium to serve the King County area. After voters defeated a stadium ballot issue in September 1966, they passed the measure as part of the Forward Thrust program in 1968. After much wrangling over its location, the Kingdome was finally completed in 1976. After more than 20 years of effort, the Seattle Seahawks made their debut as an NFL expansion team in 1976.

While the arrival of a NFL franchise in a city often means a decrease in the local college team's attendance, the Seahawks had little impact on Washington's ticket sales. When the upper deck opened on the north side of Husky Stadium in 1987, new attendance figures were set. Entering the 2004 season, Washington's games had attracted more than 70,000 fans in 90 of the 106 games played since the addition was completed..

In 1994 the Seahawks were forced to play two preseason games and three regular-season contests at Husky Stadium when the Kingdome

was temporarily closed to repair a ceiling tile problem. Two years later, when Paul Allen entered into an option to buy the Seahawks, Husky Stadium was a proposed alternative site in Allen's analysis of the purchase. Despite plans for a massive renovation of the stadium, the University again would not allow professional football to be played permanently there. Ultimately, Allen purchased the Seahawks, and a new stadium was built. During its construction, after the Kingdome was imploded in March 2000, the University agreed to rent the stadium to the Seahawks for the 2000 and 2001 seasons.

NFL teams weren't the only outsiders to rent the stadium for games. Two of the most unexpected college football games ever played at Husky Stadium took place in the early 1970s. They did not include the Huskies, but, instead, cross-state rival Washington State. Facing deficits of more than $460,000 in the early 1970s, Washington's athletic administration agreed to rent the stadium to the Cougars for a game in 1972 featuring top-ranked USC. Washington State wanted the game moved to Seattle to attract a larger crowd than possible at Martin Stadium in Pullman.

Husky coach Jim Owens was less than excited about giving Cougar coach Jim Sweeney an unfair recruiting advantage "by loaning the Cougars Husky Stadium to entertain the nation's number-one football team." It was a lopsided contest, as it turned out. Behind sophomore tailback Anthony Davis' 195 yards and

66

three touchdowns, USC routed the Cougars 44-3. After the game, Sweeney declared ruefully that WSU's play "couldn't have done much hurt to Jim Owens' recruiting program."

Two years later, WSU returned to Husky Stadium and was again beaten by a team featuring a top running back. This time it was Ohio State, with eventual two-time Heisman Trophy winner Archie Griffin, taking a resounding 42-7 victory against the hapless Cougars.

The 1990s would see Washington dominate the Pac-10. The Huskies' 82-35-1 record in the decade was easily the best in the conference. Washington players earned first-team All-Pac-10 honors 43 times during the period.

The highlight of the decade was the team's national championship in 1991. Washington entered the season ranked fourth and completely dominated its opponents, beating three top-10 teams along the way. Home games were lopsided affairs, as the Huskies outscored their six foes 287 to 47. Washington had little problem disposing of fourth-ranked Michigan, 34-14, in the Rose Bowl.

Defensive lineman Steve Emtman became the first UW player to win two major awards in the same season: the Outland Trophy and the Lombardi Trophy. He was the first pick in the NFL draft.

Between 1991 and 1993, the Washington football team won 17 consecutive games in Husky Stadium, the longest winning streak in the stadium's history. One of the victories was against a powerhouse club from Nebraska.

Above left: Quarterback Billy Joe Hobert was co-MVP in Washington's domination of Michigan in the 1992 Rose Bowl. Following the 34-14 victory, the Huskies were crowned national champions. Above right: All-American defensive tackle Steve Emtman was co-MVP in Washington's defeat of Michigan in the 1992 Rose Bowl. Emtman received the 1991 Outland Trophy and the Lombardi Trophy — the first Husky player to win two major awards in the same year.

GREAT GAMES

W

29 WASHINGTON   00:00 •••• **14** NEBRASKA

SEPTEMBER 19, 1992

A Night to Remember

Playing a rare night game, Washington posted an impressive victory against 12th-ranked Nebraska that might have provided the loudest moment in the stadium's long and boisterous history.

Late in the first quarter, Husky punter John Werdel pinned Nebraska on its three yard-line. Crowd noise caused the Husker linemen to jump offsides on consecutive plays, only adding to the frenzy of the crowd.

When Nebraska quarterback Mike Grant dropped back to his own end zone to attempt a pass, everyone in the stands watched roverback Tommie Smith blitz Grant from his blind side and drop him for a safety. The deafening roar reverberating off the twin roofs literally had the stadium rocking. An ESPN sideline reporter, armed with a noise meter, reported that the clamor reached 130 decibels.

Holding a 9-7 lead, the Husky offense went into quick-strike mode at the close of the second quarter. Speedy running back Napoleon Kaufman ended an 80-yard drive with a one-yard scoring run. Walter Bailey intercepted Grant after the kickoff, and the Huskies went for the kill. Quarterback Billy Joe Hobert threw a 24-yard scoring pass to a diving Joe Kralik to boost the lead to 23-7. Kralik appeared to be juggling the ball as he slid out of the back of the end zone, but the Huskies got the home-field call. Kicker Travis Hanson booted a pair of field goals in the second half as the Huskies posted a 29-14 win and jumped to number one in the wire service polls the following week.

The 1992 season would prove to be James' last as Husky coach. In protest of penalties placed on the program prior to the start of the 1993 season, he retired after an 18-year career. Long-time assistant coach Jim Lambright, a former all-coast player, took over just days before the season opener. Adding

emotion to Lambright's debut were the comments of Stanford coach Bill Walsh, who labeled the Huskies "mercenaries" while speaking at a booster function. When the Stanford

team plane landed in Seattle, Walsh exited wearing a pair of Groucho Marx glasses and mustache. Husky fans didn't find it very funny.

With James watching from the press box,

Above: Napoleon Kaufman races 35 yards to the Nebraska one late in the first half. He scored two plays later as the Huskies beat Nebraska 29-14. Jim Lambright (left) took the Husky coaching reins in 1993 and in four seasons compiled a 44-25-1 record.

Right: Long-time Seattle artist Stu Moldrem provided many drawings for the Washington football program beginning in the 1950s. Middle: Lawyer Milloy was a consensus All-American in 1995. He was named the nation's top defensive back by the Touchdown Club of Columbus, Ohio. Below left: Benji Olson was a consensus All-American offensive lineman in 1996 and 1997. Olson and his fellow linemen paved the way for running back Corey Dillon's school-record 1,555 yards rushing and 22 touchdowns in 1996. They also provided strong protection for quarterbacks, allowing only 18 sacks in 1996, second best in the Pac-10. In 1997, Olson helped the Huskies lead the conference in fewest sacks. Below right: A fiery team leader, Olin Kreutz was a consensus All-American center in 1997. He received the Pac-10's Morris Trophy as top offensive lineman that year and anchored a line that led the Pac-10 in fewest sacks.

Lambright had his team walk from the tunnel in tight lines, drop to one knee and raise their helmets in salute to the legendary coach. The crowd responded with emotion and roared all afternoon as the Huskies crushed the Cardinal 31-14. Lambright's teams compiled a 44-25-1 record during his six seasons. In 1995, the Huskies shared the Pac-10 title with USC.

Husky fans, who enjoy pre-game tailgate parties, may not know the history of the sprawling parking lots that surround UW's athletic complex. The north E-1 lot was originally Seattle's largest landfill, "The Montlake Dump." The University claimed the area, then wetlands, in the mid-1920's

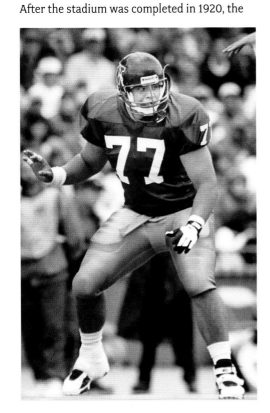

1914, the University of Washington Golf Club was organized, and its first annual meeting was held in October. A clubhouse was built and opened on New Year's Day, 1915. Eventually nine holes totaling 3,150 yards were developed, with seven holes on the west side of Montlake Boulevard and two holes east of Montlake and south of the stadium.

In 1917, the golf course became the site of the Navy Training Station. After the stadium was completed in 1920, the

and operated it as a landfill from 1926 to the early 1960s. In its latter years of operation, it received between two-fifths and two-thirds of Seattle's annual garbage. Once the landfill was covered, it became a parking lot as well as intramural playfields, Husky baseball and soccer fields, a golf driving range and a wildlife refuge.

The parking lots to the south of the stadium were built on what was once a golf course. In

40-acre area was restored to a golf course. In the early fifties, the golf course located west of Montlake became the site of the University's new Health Sciences Building. In the early 1970's, the course met its final demise when the remaining holes became parking lots and a grassy knoll along Montlake Cut.

The loyal legion of Husky fans, who arrive by foot, bicycle, bus, boat and automobile for games, enable Washington to annually lead the Pac-10 in attendance, despite the fact that Husky Stadium has only the sixth-largest seating capacity in the conference. Fans have also been known to play a role in the outcome of a game.

The most bizarre ending to a Husky Stadium game happened during the Huskies' 21-21 tie with Oregon on October 27, 1962. With the ball at midfield, Duck quarterback Bob Berry heaved it into the end zone in the direction of

Huskies faced an unranked Army team. It turned out they needed all the leather-lunged faithful to help win the game.

Relying on a triple-option rushing attack, Army jumped to a 10-0 third-quarter lead. Quarterback Damon Huard rallied the Huskies to take a 21-13 lead when the Cadets got the ball back for a final drive. Army managed to get to the Huskies' six-yard line with less than two minutes to play. With the crowd noise deafening, the Washington defense rose up to make a pair of key stops, and the Cadets could not get off a final play.

Afterward, an Army player provided one of the best descriptions of what it was like to play the Huskies on their turf. "Seventy-thousand screaming, yelling and stomping - that crowd was probably the biggest difference," said defensive tackle Al Roberts. "The acoustics here are amazing, a huge factor. I've been around C-

130 transports a lot, and this almost felt like I was on a runway." Washington's colorful defensive tackle David Richie was also awed by the crowd support. "It's always loud, but this game was really loud, especially at crunch time," he said. "When they start stomping and clapping, you can feel the metal rattle in your helmet."

Husky fans had lots to cheer the day tailback Corey Dillon rushed his way into the national record books. Playing against San Jose State in 1996, Dillon ran for 222 yards in the first quarter. That wasn't the only NCAA record he set that day. Thanks to a long screen pass, he totaled an amazing 305 all-purpose yards during 15 minutes of play. Because of the lopsided game, which the Huskies won 53-10, Dillon never returned to the game after the first quarter or he would have surely set numerous other Husky records. Later that sea-

While Spirit roams the sidelines as Washington's official mascot, you can find the Huskies' unofficial mascot, Captain Husky (below), in the southwest corner of the stadium. With a purple aviator cap, full cape and plenty of props, Captain Husky keeps fans in the spirit of the game. Captain Husky is played by Barry Erickson, who works in marketing in Seattle and is a member of the Tyee Sports Council.

wide receiver Larry Hill. As the long pass dropped from the sky, Washington's Kim Stiger went up to challenge Hill for the ball. At that exact moment, dozens of youngsters raced from their $1 bleacher seats onto the field, disrupting the play. To the dismay of Oregon, the referees let the play stand as an incompletion. Afterward, a fence was constructed behind the end zone to keep fans off the field.

With more than 4,000 participants for Washington's annual Band Day in attendance, the stadium's all-time record crowd of 76,125, was set on September 23, 1995 when the son he ran for five touchdowns against UCLA to tie McElhenny's modern-era record.

The most yards a Husky ever gained in a home game came in 1955 when running back Credell Green ran over and through Washington State for 258 yards in the Huskies' 27-7 Apple Cup victory.

One of the greatest "saves" in Husky Stadium history occurred during the 1985 Apple Cup and had nothing to do with the game itself. A late-season blizzard had dumped heavy snows on Seattle and produced such bitter-cold temperatures that anti-freeze had to be poured into stadium toilets to keep them flushing and portable heaters were placed along the sidelines. The latter nearly proved disastrous when cheerleader Marilou Franco got too close to one, and her outfit caught on fire. A quick-thinking Husky player dumped the cheerleader into a pile of snow to douse the flames that burned a baseball-sized hole in her outfit. The game was lost, but the cheerleader was spared injury.

Rick Neuheisel became Washington's 19th coach in 1999. His first teams produced a string of wild, come-from-behind victories, rallying 15 times in the fourth quarter to win games. One of the gutsiest comeback efforts was by Washington quarterback Cody Pickett in 2001. Pickett suffered a dislocated shoulder in the Huskies' October 6 victory against USC, and his status was uncertain when Washington faced Arizona two weeks later. Playing with considerable pain, Pickett passed for a school record 455 yards and then crashed through a pair of would-be tacklers in the final 10 seconds to score the game's winning touchdown in the 31-28 victory.

Washington came from behind to win games eight times in 2000 and returned to the Rose Bowl for the ninth consecutive decade. One of the rare times they kept a lead was when Miami's vaunted Hurricanes blew into Husky Stadium.

25
SUPPORT THE CURTIS WILLIAMS FUND

One of the most powerful moments in the history of the stadium came at the Nov. 4, 2000 game against Arizona when Washington dedicated the game to senior safety Curtis Williams. The previous week Williams suffered a spinal injury at Stanford that left him paralyzed. During an emotional pregame ceremony, Arizona's team joined the Washington players in saluting Williams. ABC Sports broadcast the pregame activities so that Williams could watch from his hospital room at Stanford. After falling behind 25 to 13, the Huskies rallied by scoring 22 points in the fourth-quarter to defeat the Wildcats 35-32. Williams passed away due to complications from his injury in May of 2002.

34 00:00 29
WASHINGTON •••• MIAMI

SEPTEMBER 9, 2000

The Caning of Miami

When Washington went undefeated in 1991, the team was declared national champions by the majority of organizations involved in college football rankings. The writers on the Associated Press voting board, however, picked Miami. For nearly a decade fans of the two schools argued over who had the better squad.

In 1994, the Huskies and Hurricanes finally met on the gridiron, and the underdog Washington team snapped the Canes' record 58-game home-winning streak in the Orange Bowl in a contest that became known as the "Whammy in Miami."

The 2000 game was part of a huge sporting doubleheader in Seattle. The 15th-ranked Huskies' matchup with the fourth-ranked Hurricanes led off the day, while the Seattle Mariners faced the New York Yankees in a playoff contest late in the afternoon in the Kingdome.

Washington capitalized on a fumbled Miami punt return to jump to an early lead on a scoring run by Braxton Cleman. Hurricane quarterback Ken Dorsey, playing in his first road game, had problems getting the Miami offense moving thanks to the noise created by the 74,157 in attendance.

Washington signal caller Marques Tuiasosopo clearly outplayed his counterpart, guiding the Husky offense like Patton crossing Europe. First, he bowled over several Miami defenders on a 12-yard scoring run and then tossed a touchdown pass to tight-end Jerramy Stevens to give the Huskies a 21-3 halftime lead.

Ironically, it was a Husky freshman from Miami who blew away the Hurricanes after the Canes had closed to 21-9. Neuheisel put Rich Alexis in the game "just so his parents watching in Florida knew he was doing okay." Alexis took an option toss from Tuiasosopo and raced down the Husky sideline for his first touchdown as a Husky.

Miami battled back with 13 unanswered points before Tuiasosopo engineered a long scoring drive, giving the ball to his high school teammate, Pat Conniff, for UW's final score. Tuiasosopo finished the game with 223 passing yards and 45 more on the ground. The Husky defense was magnificent, recording three sacks and recovering three fumbles.

The Huskies went on to win all their home games in 2000, post a 10-1 record and defeat Purdue in the Rose Bowl. Washington finished the season ranked third in the nation.

A year earlier, Tuiasosopo earned himself an entry in the NCAA record books while playing 25th-ranked Stanford. He overcame a first-quarter injury that left him limping much of the game to become the first college player to rush for 200 yards and pass for 300 yards in a game. The Huskies beat the Cardinal 35-30.

After the game, Husky fans gained greater appreciation for Tuiasosopo's efforts. When he appeared before the media for a post-game interview, he was on a pair of crutches, and a deep-colored bruise ran from his hip to his knee. How could he possibly accomplish such a tremendous athletic feat with so significant an

Above: Rich Alexis high-steps his way 50 yards for a touchdown in the third quarter to help the Huskies beat fourth-ranked Miami 34-29. Right: Keith Gilbertson became Washington's 24th football coach in 2003.

Quarterback Marques Tuiasosopo whips up the crowd during the 2000 Arizona game. He led the Huskies to a 35-32 come-from-behind victory in the last minute. The Huskies won seven games by a touchdown or less and trailed in eight of 10 regular season games during the 2000 season. Right: Jersey worn by Tuiasosopo.

injury? It wasn't really that bad, the quarterback said. And besides, the bruise was purple.

In 2003, Keith Gilbertson became Washington's 24th football coach, directing the Huskies to a 6-6 record. The season ended with a 27-19 victory over the Cougars, who finished ninth in the national polls.

The rich collection of stories about great players, thrilling games and colorful traditions will continue to grow as Husky Stadium advances toward its 100th anniversary. Even those who don't know the stories are awed by the structure. Visitors to the region, who see the stadium on city tours, are transfixed by its unique design and sweeping scale. Local commuters are greeted by its familiar yet striking presence as it floats above the early morning mist from Lake Washington.

Standing silent for most of the year, it awakens each autumn to embrace the football tradition it serves. The season opens with games played in the often-warm afternoons of Indian summer. October brings clear, crisp game days, with leaves turning to create a tapestry of color on the campus and surrounding neighborhood. Fans wear parkas and ponchos to big conference games in November, when the wind blows and rain causes the lighted field to gleam.

Students resume classes, and alumni return to the campus to renew old friendships. Boaters moor in Union Bay with purple and gold pennants flapping in the breeze. Lavish tailgate parties are held. Youngsters weave in and out of the crowd while walking to the stadium, imagining they are racing the length of the field for a touchdown.

Band music fills the air. Cheerleaders dance, and costumed mascots prance as purple clad fans file to their seats anticipating the excitement of the contest. The football team carries a rich heritage with it as it emerges from the stadium's tunnel, proudly wearing the purple and gold, ready to cinch up a chinstrap and continue the Husky tradition of exciting, hard-nosed football.

Since the stadium's dedication, Washington has played 84 seasons on its hallowed grounds. Teams have battled their way to 13 conference championships and 30 bowl appearances. Husky legends include 142 All-Americans, 18

consensus All-Americans, two NFL Hall of Fame members and 14 College Football Hall of Fame inductees, including four coaches. Since the stadium opened, more than 21 million have attended home games.

The true meaning of Husky Stadium, though, lies in more than statistics. It is a place of indelible memories of big moments, big games and big seasons. It is a gathering spot where the passion of players and fans fuse to ignite a joyous explosion of enthusiasm and fellowship.

Included in the stadium dedication program in 1920 was a passage that read: "It is more than a Stadium, a structure of concrete and steel. It is Washington's spirit, magnanimous in victory, invincible in defeat, a living reminder that the call of Alma Mater will always find response in the hearts of her sons and daughters."

Long after they were written, those words still ring true. —By Jim Daves and Tom Porter

Game Day by the Lake

by Jim Daves

At the edge of Lake Washington in the predawn hush of Saturday morning, the charging pulse and colorful rituals of game day at Husky Stadium come slowly to life. Faintly visible in the dim light, orange cones and directional signs are strategically placed by the parking staff to steer the tens of thousands of fans who will descend on the lots in a few more hours, transforming Montlake into a bustling, mid-sized city.

A trickle of vendors and concessionaires arrive at the cavernous stadium, unlock their stands to inventory their supplies and begin preparation for feeding and selling souvenirs to the throng known as The Husky Nation. In break rooms around the stadium, facility work crews huddle with steaming cups of coffee, their conversation turning from the operations schedule to the Huskies' chances for the day.

On the shore of Lake Washington Brandie Hassing stands on the dock of the Waterfront Activities Center. Armed with a walkie-talkie, she strains for sight of the first boat to slip through the early-morning mist. Skippers of small shuttles await her orders to assist with moorage and transport fans from their boats to the dock for the game.

"When it gets busy, it gets busy fast,"

Hassing says. "It's nice to get there early when the sun is just coming up. It's beautiful and very serene out there. It's exciting to see the first boat coming across the lake. We see a lot of the visiting teams' fans who come down to take a look. They're pretty impressed. I think everyone wishes they had the same environment — that they could come to their football games by boat. They're envious of it."

Around 6 a.m., technicians, engineers and production assistants from network television crews make their way to the TV truck pad to begin the intricate arrangements for broadcasting the game. A few hours later, producers, directors and the on-air talent will join them.

"It's very quiet at that time in the morning, a real contrast to game time," says J.R. Dexter, a regular on the Fox Sports broadcast crew. "On those clear days you cannot wait for the sun to rise. That's such a nice scene."

As the sky above the Cascade Mountains turns from black to warm orange, the pace begins to quicken. The first wave of fans arrives by land and water. Massive recreational vehicles lumber into E-1 parking lot. Outdoor grills spark to life, and the great American ritual of tailgating begins.

In the large stadium parking lots, tailgate parties run the gamut of culinary offerings, from hearty grilled sausages and meaty burgers to alder-plank smoked salmon and Dungeness crab. As you walk through the crowd, the scene feels like an outdoor concert with the Husky pregame radio show as entertainment. Some enterprising fans mount portable satellite dishes to catch the day's early games.

Back on the water, tailgating boasts an added dimension and even has its own name. Sterngating is a unique experience for the thousands who attend the game by watercraft. On a nice day, as many as 500 ships will drop anchor in the harbor just east of the stadium. Large charter boats will carry as many as 3,000 more fans to the site.

From their small pleasure craft to sea-going yachts, Lake Washington sterngaters provide one of the most unusual and attractive backdrops to a college football game in America.

"For 18 years I heard fans describe how wonderful the experience was," says former Husky coach Don James, who came to his first game as a fan by boat. "I knew enough people that had boats that I figured I would do it. We had a great time. I remember having to walk over 15 or 20 boats because of the way they stacked them. That was a lot of fun. You get up close with a lot of other people. It was every-

thing I had always heard."

Football and food are a natural combination, and fans that choose not to tailgate have plenty of options for appeasing their appetite at Husky Stadium. Concessions serve savory fare from hot dogs and chips to teriyaki, barbecue and Ivar's world-famous clam chowder. And it wouldn't be a Husky game if fans could not enjoy a latte from one of the stadium's numerous Starbucks stands.

While revelry around the stadium cranks up another notch, the mood inside the locker rooms and training rooms is altogether different as focused preparation begins for the arrival of the teams.

In the Washington locker room, equipment managers carefully lay out gear at the players' wall lockers. Jerseys, pants, pads, socks and a copy of the game-day program are all neatly arrayed. Polished helmets with a fresh set of decals rest on large racks designated with each player's uniform number.

Zipping behind a Washington State Highway Patrol escort, a convoy of buses delivers the teams to the campus two hours before kickoff. For the visitors headquartered in Bellevue, the parting of heavy traffic on the 520-foot floating bridge to allow their passage is a remarkable experience.

"That was about the most impressive thing I have ever seen," said former Notre Dame coach Lou Holtz of his team's trip to the stadium. "I saw those cars and never thought we would make it for kickoff. Everyone just pulled over, and we just drove right by."

As players file through the rear entrance of Bank of America Arena into their locker room, their looks are fixed, many of them listening to music through headphones.

"There's not a lot of screaming and shouting," says Husky equipment manager Tony Piro. "Just guys getting ready to go to work. I think people who do see it are surprised that it is not like Hollywood. Guys are not in there screaming and shouting and banging lockers and punching the walls."

"I take about 45 minutes just to stretch when I first get to the locker room," says Husky offensive tackle Khalif Barnes. "I put on a pair

of shorts and listen to some music. I do a lot of visualization. I try to play the entire game out. I try to get to a stage where I'm mellow and not over-excited. If you get too pumped up, you start to rush things and forget some of the things that are important to your preparation."

Inside the training room the staff, dressed in purple golf shirts and khaki pants, goes about the business of taping ankles, applying heat packs and helping athletes with their stretching routines.

"The atmosphere is quiet for the most part," says athletic trainer Kevin Messick. "We turn off the radios, we turn off the televisions. We try to cut down on any disturbances. Some players are very intense. Some are very relaxed. I try to look some of the key players in the eye to see if I can gauge their readiness."

As the Huskies quietly gather in their locker room, the doors to Dempsey Indoor are opened, and fans start their own pregame rituals. The party atmosphere is in sharp contrast to the solitude of the locker room cubicles.

Overnight, Dempsey Indoor had made the transition from practice field to site of the Northwest's largest tailgate party. Fans decked from head to toe in purple and gold make their way through buffet lines and gulp an assortment of beverages. Speakers blare the pregame radio show as the Husky Honks provide colorful commentary on the expectant battle. Soon the Husky marching band arrives and, to the delight of more than 2,000 fans, belts out such traditional favorites as "Tequila" and "Louie, Louie." Their 30-minute, high-voltage performance ends with a stirring rendition of "Bow Down to Washington."

Just a short walk from the locker rooms, another pair of teams prepares to play the first game of the day. At 10:15 a.m., two little league squads are escorted through the stadium, up the tunnel and into Washington's auditorium-style team meeting room. There, former Husky lineman Dan Eernissee welcomes them to Washington.

"We try to give them a feel for Husky football by doing a talk and a Q-and-A session before we take them back down to the field for their game," Eernissee says. "This has been

going on for a long time. I remember coming to (Husky) games in the '70s, and they had the little league games back then. I never get tired of watching them play. They are so enthusiastic to be on the field, even if it's just for a short period of time. It's more like a scrimmage, but to them it is like a playoff game."

As the little leaguers run through their plays, the press box operation moves into full gear. Student interns set out telephone sets and programs stuffed with game notes, rosters and depth charts. In the command center, Tom Long enters the day's announcements for the message boards, while Tony Dickinson checks the operation of the game clock and scoreboard.

In the public address booth, Lou Gellermann reviews the scripts for the pregame activities and in-game announcements. He runs through a sound check and then, along with his longtime spotters, Rick Smidt and Bob Sifferman, reviews pronunciations with the visiting school's sports information director.

In the radio booths, engineers ready equipment while Bob Rondeau and Chuck Nelson prepare to take the handoff from their respective pregame counterparts. Notes and insightful information are highlighted and taped on the booth walls for quick reference during the game.

As the little leaguers race up and down the field, the first players emerge from the tunnel. By 11:20 a.m., they have the field to themselves and begin their warm-up routines. Calisthenics lead to position drills, which eventually become a series of full-scale plays. When the stadium clock counts down to 20 minutes before kickoff, the two teams jog back up the tunnel for their final preparations.

No sooner do the players leave the stadium than Washington's marching band, massed in the east end zone, high-steps on the field to the strains of "Victory for Washington." For the next 12 minutes, band members parade through a variety of formations paying tribute to the theme of the day.

Clad in neat, purple-trimmed uniforms, members of the student band end their routine with the traditional formation of a flagpole and the unfurling of a gigantic American flag to the drum

roll and soaring music of the national anthem.

"For most bands it is a formality, something they have to do," says Husky band director Dr. Brad McDavid of the playing of the anthem. "We treat it as something special. We want to make sure it is one of the best things that we do. From the start of "Grand Old Flag," to "America the Beautiful" to "The Star-Spangled Banner," it takes up a good portion of our pregame show, and rightfully so. It is something that really tugs at the heartstrings of all Husky fans."

Stadium gates open 90 minutes before kickoff, and slowly fans walk through the turnstiles, picking up a free game program at the vestibules and making their way to their seats. The early arrivals, many wearing headphones to listen to the pregame radio show, stretch out, thumb through the program or a newspaper, watch the warmups and strike up conversation with neighbors as they arrive. With little change in the season ticket base from year to year, long-time friendships among fans are established.

As kickoff approaches, the numbers that pass through the stadium's gates swell from a stream to a noisy river. The pace accelerates as an armada of Metro buses lines Montlake Avenue, disgorging passengers. More than 15,000 spectators take the mass-transit shuttle to Washington's home games.

"We have a lot of the same fans attending the games, so they know what they are doing, and they know what to expect," says Washington Associate Athletic Director Chip Lydum. "You try to think of the crowd as one person at a time. You try to gauge their concerns and experiences, positive or negative, and see if that can be expanded to an experience that 72,000 people might be having."

Inside the Husky locker room as game time nears, emotions that players have kept carefully in check begin to rise to the surface.

"Everybody gets ready in a different way," tackle Khalif Barnes explains. "Some guys get more hyped up; some are more mellow. You have to let people get ready the way they want to. You have to respect one another. It would be like messing with a pit bull when it is getting

ready to eat. If you bother it, it might turn on you. I let the other players do what they need to do to get ready to play their best game."

The Huskies gather in their team room about 10 minutes before taking the field. The coaches give last-minute instructions as they await the referee's signal to take the field.

"By the time we did our last drill at the hotel, the coaching was basically done. At that point you knew what you were doing," says former Husky All-American Steve Emtman, who serves as a strength coach for the team. "The focus was always quiet right until the end. Right until you hit the tunnel. For a player, there is a lot of buildup that day. You have to hold yourself back from getting too excited and to save your energy. When you finally hit that tunnel, it just kind of explodes on you."

As the team spills out of its assembly room and marches toward the mouth of the tunnel, Lou Gellermann in the public address booth formally greets Husky faithful in the stands with his familiar call: "HELLO, DAWG FANS!"

The announcement ignites the stadium. The Husky band forms a passage for the team to run through. The crowd noise grows louder and is amplified when the team emerges from the tunnel. Players bunch up and begin to jump up and down like dozens of pogo sticks. Husky head coach Keith Gilbertson stands in front and, with a quick wave, sends his team onto the field to a roar from the standing crowd. Ahead of the pack race the Husky mascot, Spirit, and his handlers. A traditional blast of an air-raid siren screams through the stadium.

It's time to play ball. A week of preparation and practice culminate in the kickoff. For the next three-and-a-half hours, two teams do battle.

"When you step across the line, it is just you and the opponent," says former Husky offensive guard Pete Kaligis, who directs the Husky conditioning program. "You don't notice the fans or anything else around you. They tend to get quieter when the offense is on the field. It's like tunnel vision."

Playing in Husky Stadium gives Washington a decided advantage.

"We have a great fan base," says wide

receiver Reggie Williams. "They're really loyal. Regardless of who we're playing, they're there, and they can get really loud. That's the best part of Husky Stadium — the fans."

"The crowd just magnifies the intensity that you already have," Emtman says. "When you make a big play, all that excitement just gives you more energy. Sometimes I had a hard time hearing our calls, and I know it was brutal on the other guys. It motivated you as a player. You could watch an offense melt down in front of you."

The emotion affects more than just the players. On the sidelines, Abner Thomas, a long-time aid in the football office, bellows his familiar refrain of "Move the chains" to encourage Washington's offense.

As the team executes plays on the field, the Husky cheer squad works in front of the university's student section. Leading cheers, performing stunts and dancing to the songs of the marching band, they gyrate their way through an energetic, four-hour workout as spirited ambassadors of the school.

When a Husky player crosses the end zone, a flurry of activity ensues. High up in the radio booth, Bob Rondeau apprises his regional audience with a rousing call of "TOUCHDOWN, WASHINGTON." A band assistant sounds the air-raid siren. Replays jump to life on the big-screen scoreboard. Cheerleaders scramble aboard the helmet car for a victory lap on the stadium's track. Harry the Husky climbs atop a wooden platform and does pushups for each Washington point as students, in a jubilant chorus, count off his efforts.

As the game draws to a close and final minutes wind off the clock toward another Husky victory, the mood on Washington's sideline lightens considerably. Helmets are off and smiles are everywhere among the players. They give each other massive bear hugs and thunder-clapping high fives, the tension and focus on their faces washed away by the sweat of success.

When the clock shows no time left, they cross the gridiron to congratulate their opponents, often seeking out a former high school teammate or hometown friend. As they slowly walk off the field, the Husky alumni band forms

parallel lines to serenade them with "Bow Down to Washington" one final time.

Fans jockey for a prime spot along the Husky tunnel as the players exit the field, stopping momentarily to toss game gloves or sweat bands to the cheering throng. A small piece of equipment becomes a prized souvenir to a young Husky fan.

"The first time I came off the field I heard them yelling my name out, but I didn't know why," recalls Husky wide receiver Charles Frederick. "At first I didn't know if it was all right to throw things to the crowd, but then I saw some of the other players doing it. You try to get it to the kids because they get so excited when they catch a sweatband or a glove. It's a pretty cool thing."

"It's cool that the fans have so much interest in you," Reggie Williams says. "It's kind of funny to see how excited people get about a glove. I always try to make sure a little kid gets mine."

As the band takes the field for one final performance, fans file back to the cars, boats, bikes and buses that brought them to Husky Stadium. They tune into the postgame radio show to hear the announcer's reaction and await comments from the players and head coach.

The players gather in the team room, and Coach Gilbertson addresses their effort. Following a team prayer, he reminds them to praise their opponent to the news media, enjoy the victory and avoid doing anything foolish while celebrating with teammates and fellow students. He tells them to be ready for practice on Monday for next week's game and then calls on one of the players to lead the team's traditional postgame cheers.

After meeting with recruits and the media and conducting a post-game interview on the radio network, Gilbertson treks off to the Fifth Quarter at Dempsey Indoor where Husky supporters await his comments on the game.

The locker room, which is subdued before the game, is full of sounds as hip-hop blares from the speakers and teammates recount their performances. Assistant coaches weave between the rows of lockers, offering congratulations and providing quick feedback. A select

few players are rounded up by the media relations staff and escorted back to the team room for interviews.

As the players enjoy a hot shower, the equipment staff scours the locker room for equipment and uniforms.

Quarterback Cody Pickett and receiver Reggie Williams are the last to leave the locker room. As standout players, they know they have an obligation to talk to reporters after every game. They walk out the back door of the locker room recalling specific plays and head in separate directions, each finding his family and friends, who wait outside a temporary gate. The players' day is finally over.

Back in the stadium, sea gulls circle in search of scraps of food left in the stands. On the field, two fans clad in purple sweatshirts and Husky hats throw a football, pretending they are making the big plays that led Washington to victory.

In the Don James Center, a lone delivery man drops off boxes of pizza for members of the media, who have moved to the donor area now littered with discarded popcorn, programs and soft drink cups. They'll pound out stories and transmit them back to their news offices. The next day everyone can read their analyses of the game.

For those fortunate enough to attend games at Husky Stadium, the experience extends beyond the sidelines and end zones. Game day by the lake is an unforgettable part of life for Husky players and their legion of loyal fans. The images and sensations of the afternoon endure as time marches on.

"You respect the experience when you are playing, but you appreciate it more when you're done," former All-American Steve Emtman says. "You go through life and you realize that there is really nothing else that can match that excitement of going out of the tunnel and onto that field. Playing in front of 70,000 people and just hearing the place erupt; there's nothing you can do in life to compare with that. That's the one thing you notice when you are done playing. You can try and find that rush somewhere else, but it doesn't exist."

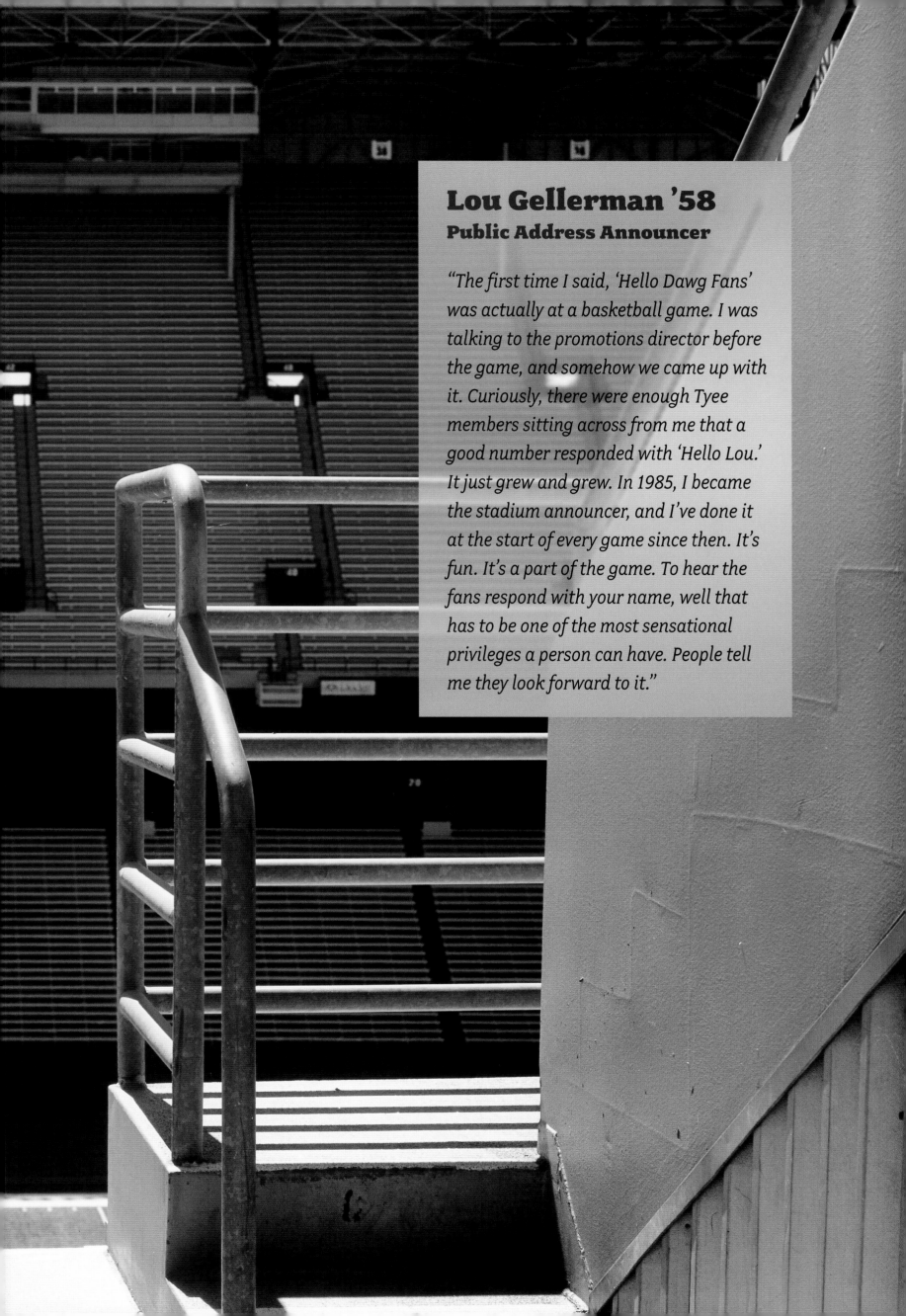

Lou Gellerman '58
Public Address Announcer

"The first time I said, 'Hello Dawg Fans' was actually at a basketball game. I was talking to the promotions director before the game, and somehow we came up with it. Curiously, there were enough Tyee members sitting across from me that a good number responded with 'Hello Lou.' It just grew and grew. In 1985, I became the stadium announcer, and I've done it at the start of every game since then. It's fun. It's a part of the game. To hear the fans respond with your name, well that has to be one of the most sensational privileges a person can have. People tell me they look forward to it."

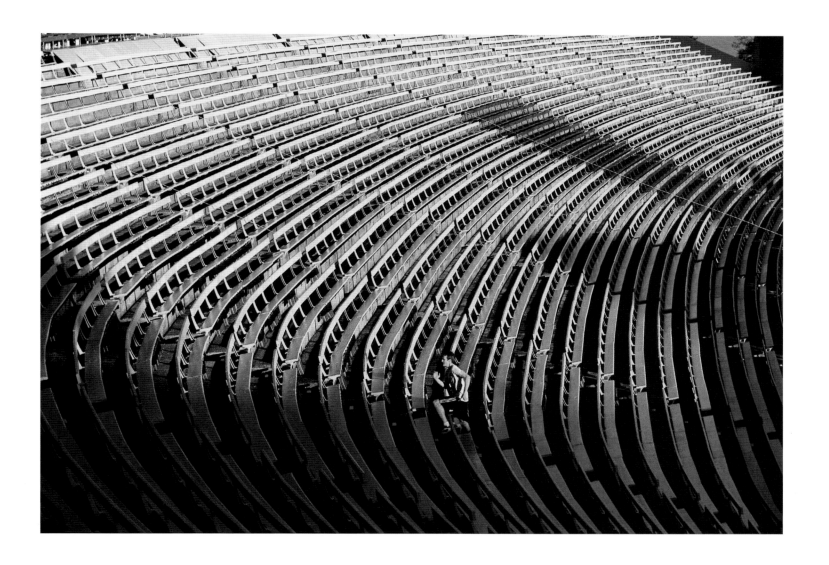

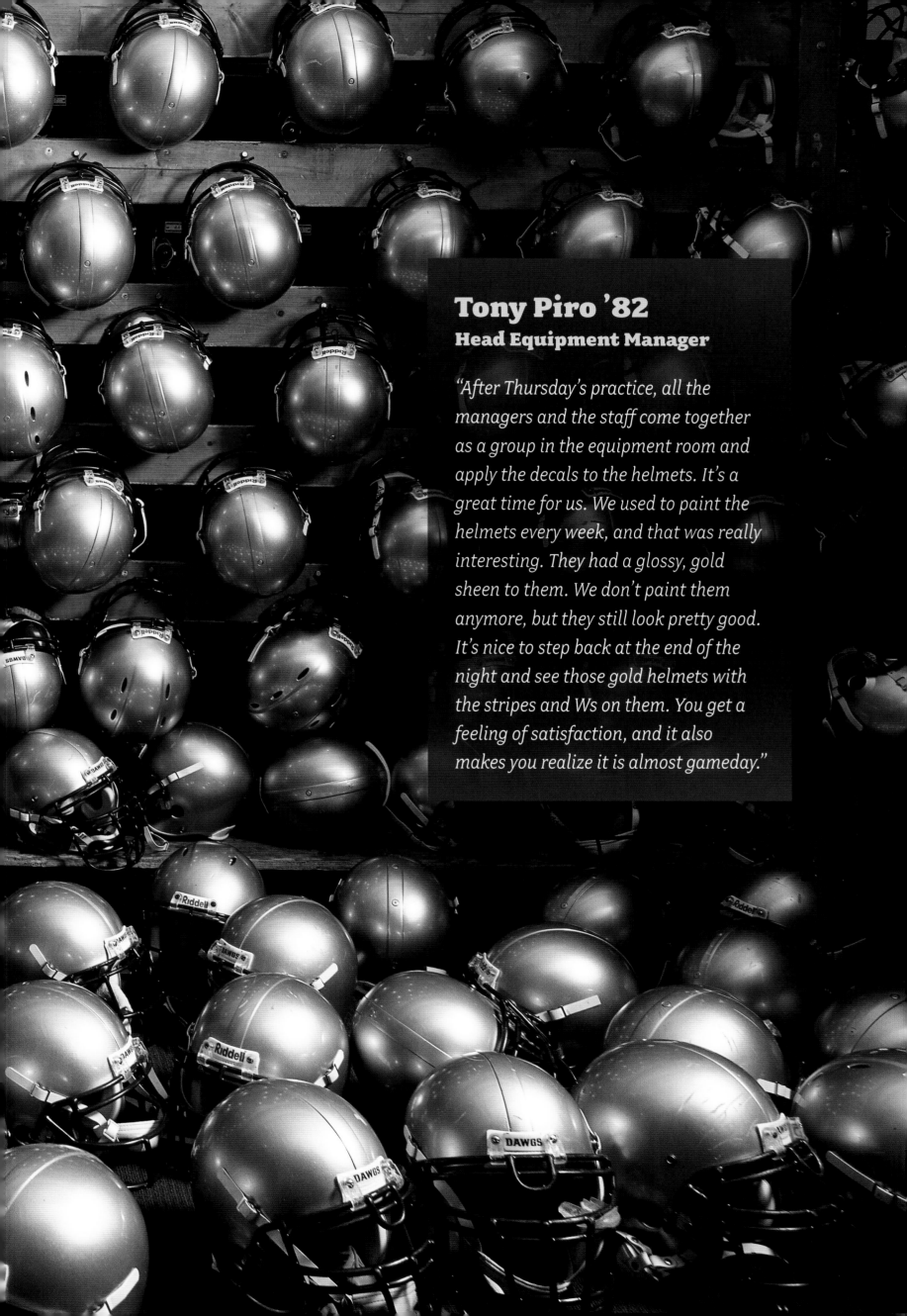

Tony Piro '82
Head Equipment Manager

"After Thursday's practice, all the managers and the staff come together as a group in the equipment room and apply the decals to the helmets. It's a great time for us. We used to paint the helmets every week, and that was really interesting. They had a glossy, gold sheen to them. We don't paint them anymore, but they still look pretty good. It's nice to step back at the end of the night and see those gold helmets with the stripes and Ws on them. You get a feeling of satisfaction, and it also makes you realize it is almost gameday."

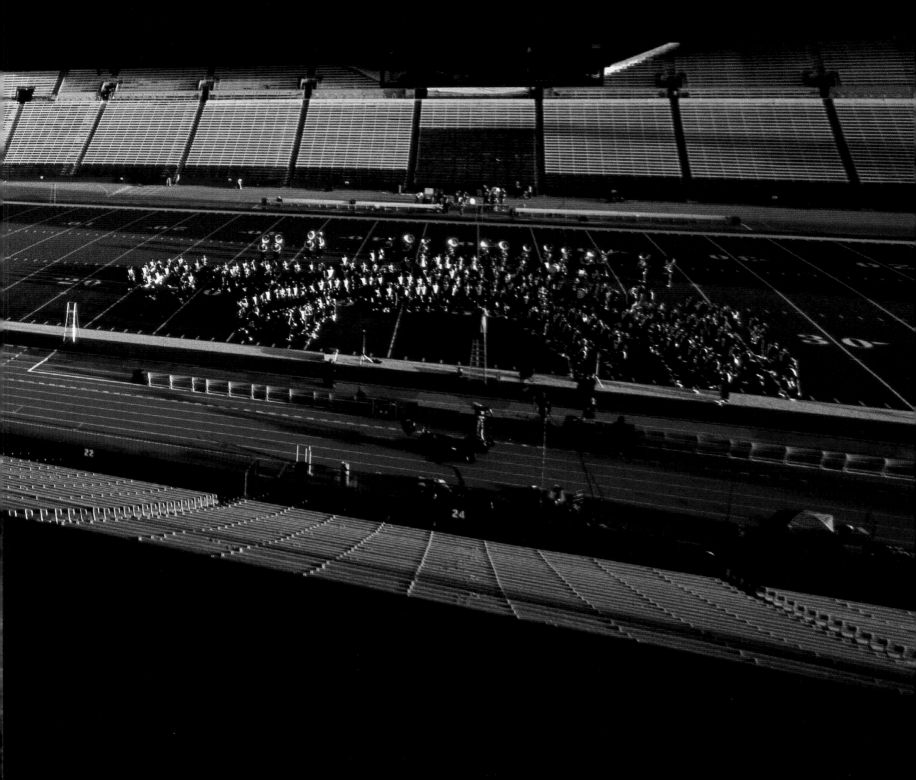

Gregg Munro
Float Plane Pilot

"It's really a beautiful stadium from the air. It's even more spectacular to see it with a crowd in the stadium. Back in the early days, we used to be able to fly right over the stadium during the games. The FAA won't let us do that anymore. We used to try and check out the scoreboard from the air to see who was winning. My folks would always be at the games when I was out flying, and I thought, 'I'll just drop by and see if I can check out the score on the way back to Kenmore.'"

Kim Cross and Spirit
Mascot Handler

"When we get close to the Stadium and the dogs see all of the people around, they start to get excited. They know something's happening. Spirit is much more that way than some of the other dogs. When my son, Ryan, takes him down to the tunnel to wait for the team to come out, Spirit is just going bananas down there. He's almost uncontrollable, he's so excited. He's bouncing around and barking and can't wait to take off. I think he knows he is a part of the show."

WASHINGTON   HUSKIES

Barry Erickson '86
Captain Husky

"After I graduated I bought season tickets in Section Eight with my pals. Someone dared me to try my old spell-out from my days as a sax player in the band. I attempted it, and it has just grown and grown. The costumes and all of that came later. I just think it's cool that people appreciate a tradition, regardless of what that tradition really is. I'm just impressed that the fans, week in and week out, follow the spell-out. What I do is not that impressive. The fact people follow it, is."

We gratefully acknowledge the following sources for the photography and memorabilia included in the history section of this book:

University of Washington Media Relations Department and its photographers including Barry Broman, Joe Freeman, Joanie Komura, Bruce Terami, Corky Trewin, and the Linkletter Studio; artists Bob McCausland and Stu Moldrem; collectors Dr. Ray Cardwell, Jim Daves, Dave Eskenazi, and Dr. Lawrence Skinner; and various Tyee yearbooks. *Sports Illustrated* covers on p. 47 © 1960 Phil Bath and on p. 53 © 1971 Fred Kaplan, are used by permission of *Sports Illustrated*. Some photographs were taken from *The Glory of Washington: The People and Events That Shaped the Husky Athletic Tradition* and *The First Century at the University of Washington*. The photo on p. 134 is © Ted S. Warren, Associated Press.

The *Seattle Times* provided permission to use photographs on the following pages:

p. 59 ... Paul Skansi's diving catch; photographer Chris Johns

p. 63 ... Greg Lewis' run; photographer Greg Gilbert

p. 63 ... Goodwill Games' opening ceremonies; photographer Harley Soltes

p. 68 ... Napoleon Kaufman's run; photographer Greg Gilbert

p. 72 ... Rich Alexis' run; photographer Steve Ringman

University of Washington Manuscripts, Special Collections, and University Archives provided the following negatives:

p.1 .... Negative UW 6655

p. 4 and 5 ...... Negative UW 1874

p. 6 .... Negative UW 1873

p. 7 .... Negative UW 1875

p.11 .... Negative UW 8493

p. 14 and 15..... Negative UW 4691

p. 20 .... Negative UW 920

                  Negative UW 20721

p. 22 and 23 .... Negative UW 1508

p. 23 .... Negative UW 1503

p.24........... Negative UW 19930

p.26........... Negative UW 23026

p.26........... Negative UW 23027

The Museum of History and Industry provided photographs from its collection on the following pages: p. 18 and 19; its Pemco Webster & Stevens Collection on p. 30 and 37; and its *Seattle Post-Intelligencer* Collection on p. 46.

Alma Mater

To her we sing who keeps the ward
    O'er all her sons from sea to sea;
Our Alma Mater, Washington,
    A health! a health! we give to thee.
Child of the mighty western land,
    You're the mother of a mighty race;
Silent her gentle vigil holds,
    In strength and purity and grace.

Chorus
All hail! O Washington!
    Thy sons and daughters sing glad acclaim
Through years of youth and loyalty;
    And still in age we sing thy fame.
In honor thy towers stand,
    Thy battlements shine in dawning light
And glow again in sunset rays.
    All hail! O Washington!